Etcetera

By E. E. Cummings

In Liveright paperback

The Enormous Room

Etcetera

is 5

No Thanks

Selected Poems

Tulips & Chimneys

22 and 50 Poems

ViVa

XAIPE

In Liveright clothbound

Complete Poems 1904–1962

Etcetera

The Unpublished Poems

E. E. CUMMINGS

Edited by
George James Firmage
and
Richard S. Kennedy

———

Together with
Uncollected Poems

edited by
George James Firmage

Liveright

New York • London

Printed in the United States of America.

For information about permission to reproduce selections from this book,
write to Permissions, W.W. Norton & Company, Inc.,
500 Fifth Avenue, New York, NY 10110.

Library of Congress Cataloging in Publication Data

Cummings, E. E. (Edward Estlin), 1894–1962.
    Etcetera: the unpublished poems / E.E. Cummings; edited by
George James Firmage and Richard S. Kennedy.
        p. cm.
    Revision of 1983 ed. including 36 additional poems.
    ISBN 0-87140-176-2 (pbk.)
        I. Firmage, George James. II. Kennedy, Richard S. III. Title.
    PS3505.U334 A6 2000b
    811′.52—dc21

                                                                00-039117

Liveright Publishing Corporation
500 Fifth Avenue, New York, N.Y. 10110
www.wwnorton.com
W. W. Norton & Company Ltd.
10 Coptic Street, London WC1A 1PU

            3   4   5   6   7   8   9   0

CONTENTS

Experiments with Typography, Spacing, and Sound, 1916–1917

Reflections of the War, Paris, Imprisonment, New York, Peace, 1918

Late Poems, 1930–1962

Appendices

Uncollected Poems

Introduction
by
Richard S. Kennedy

When E. E. Cummings died in 1962, he was, next to Robert Frost, the most popular contemporary poet in the nation and, beyond Frost, the most vociferous exponent of American individualism in the U.S. literary scene. For poetry lovers, then, the present volume is a dream of buried treasure come true. It is a stroke of good fortune when a body of unpublished work can be unearthed that represents the development of both a unique poetic style and a lively literary personality, and when it happens to be one of the leading innovators of modern poetry, we can all rejoice. The previously unpublished poems included in this volume, discovered in the three principal collections of Cummings's manuscripts at Harvard, Yale, and the University of Texas, have been selected from more than 350 unpublished pieces that the search turned up.

It turns out to be, on the whole, a collection of youthful poems, supplemented in the appendices by verses that date from E. E. Cummings's childhood and boyhood. Youthful poems for three reasons: first, because, by chance, two groups of them (those left with Elaine Orr and those found among the *Dial* papers) lay in other hands untouched and forgotten for years; second, because Cummings saved the traditional poems he wrote as a college student at Harvard and many of the exciting experiments he carried out in 1916 when he first dared to try "unpoetic" motifs and to reach for unique visual expression by his unusual spacing and alterations of typographical conventions.

But even those poems that come from the 1920s and later convey a youthful spirit most of the time. They exhibit Cummings's joyous celebration of love or express an ingenuous delight in common natural phenomena: the silent presence of the observing moon, the hushed arrival of descending snowflakes, the amazing vitality of insects, the wonder-inducing appearance of the stars.

The poems have been arranged in a rough chronological order that displays the gradual development of Cummings as a poet, except that the earliest verse has been placed in the appendices. The poems in Appendix A are taken from a little school composition book in which the young poet, age twelve, gathered his first volume of verse: seventeen poems that he carefully chose from verses written during the previous two years. They are poems we might expect from the child of a Unitarian minister living in Cambridge, Massachusetts, near the turn of the century, verses that deal with family, nation, religion, and nature. These same subjects are further developed in poems from his high-school years, in form and expressive manner reminiscent of the New England "Household Poets" whose work he was taught to revere: Longfellow, Lowell, and Emerson. A representative selection is printed in Appendix B.

By the time young Cummings entered Harvard he was writing skillfully executed verse worthy of publication in the college literary magazines, but a real turning point in his maturing took place in his sophomore year as he worked on translations from Horace, the best of which are included in Appendix C. At about the same time he began to show an awareness of a wide range in the English poetic tradition: Tennyson and Keats at first, later all the Romantics and Elizabethans, finally Rosetti, Swinburne, and the Decadents of the 1890s, who were very popular with the Harvard aesthetes of the time. After he discovered free verse both in French and in the American Imagists, he turned toward the modern movement as he found it in Amy Lowell's Imagist anthologies and the little magazines of the time, *Poetry, Others,* and *Blast.* At the same time, he went through a personal rebellion against the atmosphere of Unitarian piety at home and the decorous ethos of Cambridge in general. "In Healey's Palace," which shocked his versification teacher, shows the prevailing spirit that accompanied his creative jump into unconventional forms and subject matter during the later part of 1916 after he had left Harvard.

If we know that Cummings was a painter as well as a poet, we can easily understand his quickening interest in the visual presentation of a poem on the page—and especially if we know that he became swept up into the movements in modern painting when the Armory Show, with its European Post-Impressionist and Cubist paintings and sculptures, visited Boston in 1913. Willard Huntington Wright's *Modern Art* became his favorite reading, and Cézanne the painter he admired most. Soon Duchamp, Picasso, and Brancusi became saints in his religion of art. By 1917, Cummings was living in New York trying seriously both to develop himself into a Cubist painter and to find a new way of writing poetry.

These were the cultural forces that helped to shape Cummings's distinctive style. When the United States entered the war, social forces made their impact, too, especially in hardening the attitudes that his poems express. Cummings joined the Norton-Harjes Ambulance Corps, reported for duty in Paris (where he saw Nijinski dance in Stravinsky's *Petrouchka* and attended the premiere performance of Satie's *Parade* with Cubist sets designed by Picasso), served at the front for three months, endured three months in a French concentration camp on false charges of espionage (an experience recorded in his autobiographical narrative, *The Enormous Room*), returned to wartime New York after his release, and served six months in the U. S. Army Infantry at Camp Devens before the Armistice set him free to live his own individualistic life once again.

By now, the idealized view of the world that had marked his Harvard years was hidden under a tough veneer of expression that appeared in poems about drunks, bums, prostitutes, chorus girls, and harsh urban scenery and in satires directed against politicians, generals, preachers, educators, advertisers—the whole political and social leadership of the United States and the values of its business-dominated society. But the genuine tenderness of his sensibility still peeped out in exquisite love poems addressed to Elaine Orr, the woman he loved and later married, and in poems that display a sensitive awareness of the beauties of the natural world. The "i" who spoke in his poems was not only the little man who was pushed around by authority or ground under the wheels of society but also a Pierrot whose heart yearned for his beloved or a soft-souled romantic who could feel sympathetic identification with a mouse or a chickadee. These were the years of his earliest volumes of verse, *Tulips and Chimneys*, *&*, *XLI Poems*, and *Is 5*.

There are not as many unpublished poems from the later years, the 1930s and after, because, if the Cummings papers at Harvard are a reliable guide, he no longer dashed off poems with the spontaneous frequency that was his youthful habit. He now worked slowly and carefully, through many drafts, refining his motifs and shaping his patterns. He published the results; there was not much left over. Most of his work sheets contain only unfinished poems. For example, one satirical sonnet that ends, "(Not that we object to boston / i'm inclined not to be found dead there that's all," he never brought into satisfactory shape, although he had begun it in the 1930s and continued to think about it from time to time (in later years, he mentioned to a friend that he had put away a poem about Boston that he hoped to finish some day). Sometimes he would give up on a poem and place the sheets in a folder labeled "inferior verse."

The finished poems from this period remind us of Robert Graves's comment: "most poets slowly decay; Cummings slowly matures." Marion Morehouse, Cummings's widow, withheld one poem from publication in his posthumous volume. Some erotic poems Cummings himself kept back, given no choice by the publishing standards of the time. Some others he apparently had lost track of. A few he was probably holding for further review, still weighing which of his several versions to choose (in these cases we have made the choice for him). However all this may be, the forty-three pieces published here in the final section are quite representative of Cummings's mature years and quite worthy to have been included in such later volumes as *1 × 1, XAIPE,* or *95 Poems.*

We are happy to have the opportunity to reintroduce Cummings to his readers with these works that have lain undisturbed for years but still retain their freshness. Once again he will charm, amuse, jar, and intrigue whoever picks up this volume, and sometimes, he will touch a very special place in that reader's being.

Etcetera

NOTE ON THE TEXT

The original, fair typescripts of the 166 unpublished poems selected for inclusion in *Etcetera* can be found in the following private and institutional collections:

> Nancy T. Andrews, London, England (10 poems)
> The Houghton Library, Harvard University, Cambridge, Massachusetts (135 poems)
> The Beinecke Rare Book and Manuscript Library, Yale University, New Haven, Connecticut (17 poems)
> Humanities Research Center, the University of Texas, Austin, Texas (4 poems)

Only forty-six of the poems had appeared in print before the publication, in 1991, of *Complete Poems 1904–1962*: eight as part of a collection of Cummings's work published in England in 1973; thirteen in a series of articles by Richard Kennedy published in the *Harvard Library Bulletin* in 1976 and 1977 and in the *Journal of Modern Literature* in 1979; seventeen from a manuscript entitled "8 sonnets 16 other things" that also appeared in the *Journal of Modern Literature*; and eight poems that are the "Raison d'Etre" of *Charon's Daughter*, a book by the poet's daughter issued by Liveright in 1977. Thanks are due to all the publishers involved for their permission to reprint the poems.

The texts and typographical arrangements of the poems in *Etcetera* are those of the manuscripts noted above.

GEORGE JAMES FIRMAGE

THE HARVARD YEARS
1911–1916

E. E. Cummings arrived at Harvard with some local reputation as a poet, for it was known that he had been the literary editor of the *Cambridge Review* at the Cambridge Latin School and had frequently published his verses there. During his first year, he was sought after by the editors of the rival literary magazines, the *Harvard Monthly* and the *Harvard Advocate*, who were eager to have him contribute to their pages. After publishing poems in each magazine, Cummings finally decided to join the staff of the *Harvard Monthly*, in which he published his work for the next four years. Some of these pieces later appeared in *Eight Harvard Poets* (1917), a cooperative venture of the Harvard Poetry Society, and in his first volume of poems, *Tulips and Chimneys* (1923).

But the Cummings papers at Harvard and the University of Texas contain more than two hundred unpublished poems from his Harvard years, only a sample of which we have chosen in order to illustrate his early work in both traditional forms and free verse. Most of what he turned out in these years are nature poems and love poems, but we have included a few of his literary tributes, which indicate that while he was in college he began to feel that he could become a member of the great international brotherhood of poets.

The college friends whom he addressed in the poems in part 4 should be identified. T.A.M. is Theodore A. Miller, Cummings's Greek teacher and his closest friend during the first two years of college; the occasion was his departure on a trip to Europe. S.F.D. is S. Foster Damon, who had introduced Cummings to modern poetry, art, and music, especially the work of Claude Debussy. The Watson of the third poem is James Sibley Watson, who guided Cummings's taste in modern French poetry and who later became one of the editors of *The Dial* magazine. S.T. is Scofield Thayer, another editor of *The Dial* and Cummings's closest friend in the postwar years; the occasion was Thayer's marriage to Elaine Orr, who later divorced Thayer and married Cummings.

The last poem in part 5, "In Healey's Palace," is one that shocked Cummings's professor, Dean Lebaron Russell Briggs, who taught the course in English Versification. Its vernacular robustness represents another side of Cummings that began to emerge in his final year at Harvard.

Early

I

SEMI-SPRING

A thin, foul scattering of grim, grey snow,
Reaching out scrawny limbs, deep digs its nails
Into the bleeding face of suppliant earth,
And grins with all its broken, yellow teeth.

A warm, serene, soft heaven gazes down
With dreamy eyes upon the fiend-cramped world.
The rosy eastern glow, the sun's I Come,
Patters about the sky, and coos, and smiles—
Sweet babe with tender, rose-begetting feet.

From a black corpse of tree, the hideous rasp
Of staring grackles, clucking and bowing each
In drivelling salute, splits the soft air
To inharmonious fragments; everywhere
A nervous, endless, hoarse, incessant chirp
Of sparrows telling all the evil news.

Ah, God—for the flower-air of Spring!   To see
The world in bud!   To press with eager feet
The dear, soft, thrilling green again!   To be
Once more in touch with heaven upon earth!
One soul-toned thrush's perfect harmony,
One little warbler's huge felicity,
One buttercup!   One perfect butterfly!

II

THE PAPER PALACE

A clan of imps—morose and ugly things,
　　Brown-bodies,evil-headed,slayers all,—
Has climbed the shuddering air with embryo wings
　　And from my porch's beam slowly let fall
With toil unspeakable,a fairy ball,
A palace hung in either!　Fine as cloth
　　Moon-spun on elfin loom,each filmy wall,
Light as a buoyant cloudlet's feathery froth,
Frail as a lily's face,soft as a silver moth.

III

Night shall eat these girls and boys.
Time makes his meal of thee and me.
Love a broken doll shall be;
the moon and sun like tired toys

(with all whereat joined hearts rejoice)
shall drop softly into the sea.
Night shall eat these girls and boys.
Time makes his meal of thee and me.

Love,lady,prizeth wisely thee;
whose white and little hand annoys
the universal death,pardi:
whose most white body is his voice.
Night shall eat these girls and boys.

Literary Tributes
I
CHAUCER

Kind is his mouth and smiling are his eyes,
Who rideth on that sunny pilgrimage,
And tears and laughter be his golden wage,
And that sweet carolling which never dies.
O Pilgrim of green springtide and blue skies,
Thy heart is dear to men of every age,
All sympathy is in thy withered page,
Whose soul was singing ere thy hand was wise.

'Tis not in marble that we worship thee,
But rather when the first white flower is come
To naked gardens, and immortal youth
Leaps to the world,—there shall thy worship be
In perfect simpleness and perfect truth,—
O singing soul no dying can make dumb!

Great Dante stands in Florence, looking down
In marble on the centuries.   Ye spell,
Beaneath his feet who walked in Heaven and Hell,
"L'Italia."   Here no longer lord and clown
Cringe, as of yore, to the immortal frown
Of him who loved his Italy too well:
Silent he stands, and like a sentinel
Stares from beneath those brows of dread renown.

Terrible, beautiful face, from whose pale lip
Anathema hurtled upon the world,
Stern mask, we read thee as an open scroll:
What if this mouth Hate's bitter smile has curled?
These eyes have known Love's starry fellowship;
Behind which trembles the tremendous soul.

III

FAME SPEAKS

Stand forth, John Keats!   On earth thou knew'st me not;
Steadfast through all the storms of passion, thou,
True to thy muse, and virgin to thy vow;
Resigned, if name with ashes were forgot,
So thou one arrow in the gold had'st shot!
I never placed my laurel on thy brow,
But on thy name I come to lay it now,
When thy bones wither in the earthly plot.
Fame is my name.   I dwell among the clouds,
Being immortal, and the wreath I bring
Itself is Immortality.   The sweets
Of earth I know not, more the pains, but wing
In mine own ether, with the crownéd crowds
Born of the centuries.—Stand forth, John Keats!

IV

HELEN

Only thou livest.   Centuries wheel and pass,
And generations wither into dust;
Royalty is the vulgar food of rust,
Valor and fame, their days be as the grass;

What of today?   vanitas, vanitas...
These treasures of rare love and costing lust
Shall the tomorrow reckon mold and must,
Ere, stricken of time, itself shall cry alas.

Sole sits majestic Death, high lord of change;
And Life, a little pinch of frankincense,
Sweetens the certain passing...from some sty

Leers even now the immanent face strange,
That leaned upon immortal battlements
To watch the beautiful young heroes die.

Love Poems

I

I have looked upon thee—and I have loved thee,
Loved thy mouth, whose curve is the moon's young crescent,
Loved thy beauty-blossoming eyes, and eyelids
    Petal-like, perfect;
I would brush the dew in a flashing rainbow
From thy face's twain mysterious flowers,
And, supremely throned on the lips' full luna,
    Soar into Heaven.

II

REVERIE
(A translation from Sophocles's *Electra*)

This love of ours, you of my heart, is no light thing;
For I have seen it in the east and in the west,
And I have found it in the cloud and in the clear.
Are you not with me at all times, faithfully standing,
The soul of that golden prelude which is the childhood of day,
By each imperishable stanza called a moment,
Unto the splendid close, glory and light, envoi,
Followed with stars?
                              Verily you were near to me,
To watch the strong boy-swallows carolling in sunset,
To barter day and thought for night and ecstasy,
To dream great dreams, you of my heart; to live great lives.

You are the sunset.   You are the long night of peace.
And dawn is of you, a thrilling glory frightening stars.

III

Thy face is a still white house of holy things,
Graced with the quiet glory of thy hair.
Upon thy perfect forehead the sweet air
Hath laid her beauty where girlhood clings.
Thine eyes are quivering celestial springs
Of naked immortality, and there
God hath Hope, where those twin angels stare,
That sometimes sleep beneath their sheltering wings.
The seals of love on those strong lips of thine
Are perfect still; thy cheeks await their kiss.
Thou art all virginal; God made thee His.
Lost in the unreal life, the deathful din,
Man bows himself before the Only Shrine—
Who shall go in, O God—who shall go in?

IV

What is thy mouth to me?
A cup of sorrowful incense,
A tree of keen leaves,
An eager high ship,
A quiver of superb arrows.

What is thy breast to me?
A flower of new prayer,
A poem of firm light,
A well of cool birds,
A drawn bow trembling.

What is thy body to me?
A theatre of perfect silence,
A chariot of red speed;
And O, the dim feet
Of white-maned desires!

V

DEDICATION

The white rose my soul
Is blown upon the ways.
Over the high earth
Valleys bring it forth,
And it is found upon mountains.

The white rose my soul
Knoweth all winds and wings,
All nests, all songs,
With each smiling star,
And every graceful day.

The white rose my soul
Is under the world's feet.
(Only thou dost hold,
In that how little hand,
The red rose my heart.)

VI

I love you
For your little,startled,thoughtless ways,
For your ponderings,like soft dark birds,
And when you speak 'tis a sudden sunlight.

I love you
For your wide child eyes,and fluttering hands,
For the little divinities your wrists,
And the beautiful mysteries your fingers.

I love you.
Does the blossom study her day of life?
Is the butterfly vexed with an hour of soul?
I had rather a rose than live forever.

VII

After your poppied hair inaugurates
Twilight, with earnest of what pleading pearls;
After the carnal vine your beauty curls
Upon me, with such tingling opiates
As immobile my literal flesh awaits;
Ere the attent wind spiritual whirls
Upward the murdered throstles and the merles
Of that prompt forest which your smile creates;

Pausing, I lift my eyes as best I can,
Where twain frail candles close their single arc
Upon a water-colour by Cézanne.
But you, love thirsty, breathe across the gleam;
For total terror of the actual dark
Changing the shy equivalents of dream.

VIII

Moon-in-the-Trees,
The old canoe awaits you.
He is not, as you know, afraid of the dark,
And has unaided captured many stars.

The same tent expects your coming,
Moon-in-the-Trees.
You remember how the spruce smelled sweet
When the dawn was full of little birds?

In the ears of my days
Is a thunder of accomplished rivers;
In the nostrils of my nights
An incense of irrevocable mountains.

IX

When thou art dead,dead,and far from the splendid sin,
And the fleshless soul whines at the steep of the last abyss
To leave forever its heart acold in an earthy bed,

When,forth of the body which loved my body,the soul-within
Comes,naked from the pitiless metamorphosis,
What shall it say to mine,when we are dead,dead?

(When I am dead,dead, and they have laid thee in,
The body my lips so loved given to worms to kiss,
And the cool smooth throat,and bright hair of the head—).

X

You are tired,
(I think)
Of the always puzzle of living and doing;
And so am I.

Come with me, then,
And we'll leave it far and far away—
(Only you and I, understand!)

You have played,
(I think)
And broke the toys you were fondest of,
And are a little tired now;
Tired of things that break, and—
Just tired.
So am I.

But I come with a dream in my eyes tonight,
And I knock with a rose at the hopeless gate of your heart—
Open to me!
For I will show you the places Nobody knows,
And, if you like,
The perfect places of Sleep.

Ah, come with me!
I'll blow you that wonderful bubble, the moon,
That floats forever and a day;
I'll sing you the jacinth song
Of the probable stars;
I will attempt the unstartled steppes of dream,
Until I find the Only Flower,
Which shall keep (I think) your little heart
While the moon comes out of the sea.

XI

Let us lie here in the disturbing grass,
And slowly grow together under the sky
Sucked frail by Spring,whose meat is thou,and I,
This hurrying tree,and yonder pausing mass
Hitched to time scarcely,eager to surpass
Space:for the day decides;O let us lie
Receiving deepness,
Hearing,over

The poised,rushing night ring in the brim
Of Heaven;then,perpendicular odors stealing
Through curtains of new loosened dark;and one—
As the unaccountable bright sun
Becomes the horizon—
Bird,nearly lost,lost;wheeling,wheeling.

Friends

I

T.A.M.
Sailed July, 1914

Auf wiedersehen!   We part a little while,
Friends alway, till what time we meet again.
Of this our life, the hours of sun and rain,
No palest flower the future can beguile;
Then let him frown his frown or smile his smile!
There are some things which have not lived in vain,
These which have made us men and which remain,
Tho' tide and time be lost 'twixt mile and mile.

Fear not, for thou shalt speak with me, my friend,
Who care not if this little journey's end
Lie past so great a gulf as never yields
One smallest murmur.—When the world's in sleep,
I will go out where God's white legions keep
A shining bivouac in celestial fields.

II

S.F.D.
In Memory of Claude o'Dreams

Behold, I have taken at thy hands immortal wine
The fume whereof is ecstasy of perfect pain,
Which is more sweet than flowers unknown uttered of rain,
More potent than the fumbling might of the brute of brine.
Lo, my pale soul is blown upon far peaks with thine,
Steeped in star-terrible silence, at whose feet the plain
Murmurs of thought and time's illimitable refrain,
Upon whose brows eternity setteth high sign.

This thing hath been, by grace; one music in our souls,
One fane beyond the world, whence riseth sacrifice
Unto that god whom gifts invisible appease.
So be it when sunset's golden diapaison rolls.
Over our life—then shalt thou, smiling, touch the keys,
And draw me softly with thee into Paradise.

III

Softly from its still lair in Plympton Street
It stole on silent pads, and, raping space,
Shot onward in a fierce infernal race,
And shivered townward on revolving feet,
Skidded, fortuitously indiscreet;
And now a lady doth its bosom grace,
And now the 'phone, tingling its wild disgrace,
Telleth that hearts be broke and time is fleet.

O Watson, born beneath a generous star,
Oft have I seen thee draped upon a bar;
Thou might'st have slain us with a bloody couteau
And,

      O Watson, moriturus te saluto,

Infinite in thy fair beatitude;
But you could not do anything so rude.

IV

S.T.

O friend, who hast attained thyself in her,
Thy wife, the almost woman whose tresses are
The stranger part of sunlight, in the far
Nearness of whose frail eyes instantly stir

Unchristian perfumes more remote than myrrh,
Whose smiling is the swiftly singular
Adventure of one inadvertent star,
With angels previously a loiterer,

Friend, who dost thy unfearing soul pervert
From the perfection of its constancy
To that unspeakable fellowship of Art—

Receive the complete pardon of my heart,
Who dost thy friend a little while desert
For the sensation of eternity.

Late

I

They have hung the sky with arrows,
Targes of jubilant flame, and helms of splendor,
Knives and daggers of hissing light, and furious swords.

They have hung the lake with moth-wings,
Blurs of purple, and shaggy warmths of gold,
Lazy curious wines, and curving curds of silver.

They have hung my heart with a sunset,
Lilting flowers, and feathered cageless flames,
Death and love: ashes of roses, ashes of angels.

II

A painted wind has sprung
Clean of the rotten dark,
Lancing the glutted wolves of rain.

The sky is carried by a blue assault.
Strident with sun the heights swarm,
The vasts bulge with banners.

Working angels
Shovel light in heaven.

To carnival, to carnival,
In ribbons of red fire,
With spokes of golden laughter,
God drives the jingling world.

III

You shall sing my songs, O earth.
With tilted lips and dancing throat shall you sing them,
The songs my poems.

You shall dream my dreams, O world.
Locked in the shining house of beautiful sleep,
Of the dreams my poems.

You shall smile my smile, love.
My eyes, my eyes have stroked the bird of your soul,
The bird my poems.

In Healey's Palace I was sitting—
Joe at the ivories, Irene spitting
Rag into the stinking dizzy
Misbegotten Hall, while Lizzie,
Like a she-demon in a rift
Of Hell-smoke, toured the booths, half-piffed.

I saw two rah-rahs—caps, soft shirts,
Match-legs, the kind of face that hurts,
The walk that makes death sweet—Ted Gore
And Alec Ross; they had that whore
Mary between them.   Don't know which,
One looked; and May said: "The old bitch
Lulu, as I'm a virgin, boys!"
And I yelled back over the noise:
"Did that three-legged baby croak
That you got off the salesman-bloke?"

The beer-glass missed.   It broke instead
On old man Davenport's bald head.
I picked a platter up, one-handed.
Right on her new straw lid it landed.
Cheest, what a crash!
                              Before you knew,
Ted slipped the management a new
Crisp five, and everyone sat down
But May, that said I'd spoiled her gown,
And me, that blubbered on her shoulder,
And kissed her shiny nose, and told her
I didn't mean to smash her...Crowst,
But I was beautifully soused!
I think Al called me "good old sport,"
And three smokes lugged out Davenport.

EXPERIMENTS WITH TYPOGRAPHY, SPACING, AND SOUND 1916–1917

During his last year at Harvard, Cummings became acquainted with the unconventional poetry being published in his time, in periodicals such as *Poetry, Others,* and *Blast* and in books such as Amy Lowell's *Sword Blades and Poppy Seeds,* Ezra Pound's *Cathay,* and the anthology *Des Imagistes.* In fact, Cummings delivered an address, "The New Art," during his graduation exercises in 1915, which showed that he was quite knowledgeable about the avant-garde activity in painting and music as well as in poetry. Yet he did not write any poems that reveal a radical break from conventional forms until after he finished his graduate year in 1916.

Then, during the first six months after leaving college, he played with language on his typewriter, he dabbled in Cubist painting, and he read the latest criticism on modern art and literature. He was searching for a personal style that would be unique in the modern movement. He tried out new spatial arrangements, both horizontal and vertical, for poems he had written in free verse the previous year. He composed new poems based on patterns of vowel or consonant groups. He developed linguistic constructions that dealt with what were then considered unpoetic subjects: casual conversations, banal statements, urban impressions. These creations were presented by means of a variety of voices and a range of tones, from the naïve and nostalgic to the tough and cynical. Such well-known poems as "in Just- / spring," "writhe and / gape of tortured," and "the hours rise up putting off stars and it is," which were later published in *Tulips and Chimneys,* were written during this time.

We have selected a few examples from a large body of working papers to show the kinds of constructions (he did not use the word, "poem," but chose rather the French word, "fait") that he was putting together as he was working out his own distinctive way of writing poetry. They are fascinating literary exercises, and some of them—for example, "mr. smith" and "wanta"—deserved to be published by Cummings in his early volumes rather than to have been set aside and lost among stacks of drafts and abandoned ideas.

I

The awful darkness of the town
crushes;in rows
houses every one a different shade of brown
(unity in variety,I suppose).
It almost snows:
inside,the silly people are teaing with bread-and-butter sandwiches

talking of the weather,and who
married whom
(the sons of b--s)
—thin smiles glue
the pasteboard faces,and prevent
sawdust from pouring out of this
chink or that.
The gloom
is flat,
as a poor pancake is
flat;"My dear,our church sent
three thousand bandages only last week
to those poor soldiers"—Whew!
how they reel

those sweet people.   But I'm
going into the Parthenon
to lap yaoorti with my eyes shut
tight.   Goodbye
Cambridge.   I'm going

in to see Nichol,and devour shishkabob(what
's the time?
Five? I must be moving on,
leaving the houses-all-alike
thank God)and I guess I'll drop in and get Mike
to give me a high.

II

A GIRL'S RING

the round of gold
tells me slenderly
twinkling
fauns pinkly

leapingassembled
to pipe-sob
and grappling
cymbals lunge thwart vistas

buxom
swaggering satyrs
from thousand
coverts smooth dryads

peek
eyes
trail
with merriment of spiraea

III

logeorge
    lo
      wellifitisn't eddy   how's the boy
grandhave youheard
         shoot

            you knowjim
goodscout   well

  married

  the hellyousay
      whoto

   'member ritagail
do i remember rita   what'sthejoke

             well

                 goddam

   don'ttakeit too hard old boy

sayare you kidding me   because ifyouare   byhell
  easyall george watchyourstep old fellow

  christ

    that   that

mut

IV

wee people
        dwelling
between serene
            day-
light
and

    god

       o make room for
my coming which shall be
              as
the sky comes

        down into those valleys

                 cocks cheer softly
                    a cow-bell

                    occassional
                    invisible

                    tamps
                    twilight

V

                the sky
                was   can dy
        lu   mi
                nous   ed
                            i
                ble
                    spry pinks
                    shy   lem
                ons
                                    greens
            cool
        choco   lates
                    un   der
    a   lo
            co
            mo   tive   s pout
                            ing
                    vi
            o   lets

VI

beyond the stolid iron pond
soldered with complete silence
the huge timorous hills
squat like permanent vegetables

the judging sun pinches smiling
here and there some huddling vastness
claps the fattest finally
and tags it with his supreme blue

whereat the just adjacent valley
rolls proudly his belligerent bosom
deepens his greens inflates his ochres
and in the pool doubles his winnings

mr. smith
is reading
his letter
by the fire-
light

    tea-time

        smiles friend smith

no type   bold o's
           d's gloat
           droll l's twine
           r's rove

           haha

                sweet-hearts
                part   fellow
                like   darl- write
                i dream my   try ned   ma
                thinks
                right thing   will be still
                till death
                thine

blows ring

strokes nose   P
toasts toes   S
                kiss

don't get me wrong oblivion
  I never loved you kiddo
you that was always sticking around

                        spoiling me for everyone else
                        telling me how it would make
                        you nutty if I didn't let you
                        go the distance

and I gave you my breasts to feel
didn't I
      and my mouth to kiss

  O I was too good to you oblivion old kid   that's all
  and when I might have told you

                        to go ahead and croak yourselflike
                        you was always threatening you was
                        going to do
                                I didn't
                                I said   go on you inter-
                                est me
                                I let you hang around
                                and whimper

  and I've been getting mine
Listen

there's a fellow I love like I never loved anyone else that's six
  foot two tall with a face any girl would die to kiss and a skin
  like a little kitten's
that's asked me to go to Murray's tonight with him and see the cab-
  aret and dance   you know
well
if he asks me to take another I'm going to and if he asks me to take
another after that I'm going to do that and if he puts me into a taxi
and tells the driver to take her easy and steer for the morning I'm
going to let him and if he starts in right away putting it to me in

the cab
    I'm not going to whisper
    oblivion
do you get me
    not that I'm tired of automats and Childs's and handing out ribbon to
    old ladies that ain't got three teeth and being followed home by pimps
    and stewed guys and sleeping lonely in a whitewashed room three thou-
    sand below Zero   oh no
                            I could stand that
    but it's that I'm O Gawd how tired
                               of seeing the white face of you and
                               feeling the old hands of you and
                               being teased and jollied about you
                               and being prayed and implored and
                               bribed and threatened
to give you my beautiful white body
    kiddo
            that's why

wanta
spendsix

dollars Kid
                    2 for the room
        and
                         four   for the girl
            thewoman wasnot

            quite Fourteen   till she smiled
                                                                then

Centuries   she
                                     soft ly
        repeated
        well   whadyas ay
                         dear
                         wan
                         taspend

                 six

            Dollars

X

maker of many mouths

earth

why yet once more pronounce
                        for the poor entertainment of
                        eternity

this old impertinence
   of the always unimportant

                    poet
                    death

   tree capable of spring

how does consent the genius of thy beauty
                                haggard with re-
                                hearsal

unprotestingly to take
   these uninspired lines

                    for whom

   unto what god acceptable

dost thou pronounce
indifferently
                o prompted sky

        mechanical gold

REFLECTIONS OF THE WAR, PARIS, IMPRISONMENT, NEW YORK, PEACE 1918

The poems in this section have been selected from a large number that Cummings wrote after his return from wartime France and the imprisonment in *The Enormous Room*, some of them written during his six months of service in the U.S. Army at Camp Devens, Massachusetts. This is the period that saw the composition of some of the best work that later appeared in *Tulips and Chimneys, &,* and *LXI Poems* and some of the most sexually intense (as well as some of the most sexually cynical) poems in those volumes.

A few of the poems chosen for this section may be better understood if we know that in Paris Cummings had become acquainted with a number of French prostitutes—indeed, had become quite attached to one named Marie Louise Lallemand before he went to the battle front—but he had maintained his virginity until the night before he sailed home to the United States. After his release from the French concentration camp, he had been unable to find Marie Louise in Paris and turned then to a woman named Berthe, a waitress at his favorite restaurant, Sultana Cherque's Oasis. At least two of the poems included here refer specifically to that experience.

The poem "a Woman / of bronze" appears to be his ironical comment on the curtailment of civil liberties during the war. "Noise" is his impression of the joyous outburst at the premature announcement of the Armistice—and is composed in the wrenching style that Cummings conceived of as analogous to Cubism in painting.

I

along the justexisting road to Roupy
little in moonlight
go silently by men
(who will be damned if they know why)

où va-tu, Than-Time-Older with
wish-bones legs & the five bidons?
women in your eyes,
death on your shoulder

c'est madame de la guerre
with love-slovenly
mouth,
who has turned his mouth from
the crisp bright mouths of girls

the arms of wives are crying
& crying:you have taken the arms
which held us roughly and gently
madame de la Mort,we do not know you
and we hate you!

whither goest thou
Might Be Older
(death on your shoulder
women in your eyes?)

through the tasteless minute efficient room
march hexameters of unpleasant
twilight,a twilight smelling of Vergil,
as me bang(to and from)
the huggering rags of white Latin flesh
which her body sometimes isn't
(all night,always,a warm incessant gush
of furious Paris flutters up the hill,
cries somethings laughters loves nothings float
upward,beautifully,forces crazily rhyme,
Montmartre s'amuse!obscure eyes hotly dote
....as awkwardly toward me for the millionth time
sidles the ruddy rubbish of her kiss
i taste upon her mouth cabs and taxis.

|||

my deathly body's deadly lady

smoothly-foolish exquisitely,tooled
(becoming exactly passionate Gladly

grips with chuckles of supreme sex

my mute-articulate protrusion)
Inviting my gorgeous bullet to vex

the fooling groove intuitive...

And the sharp ripples-of-her-brain bite
fondly into mine,
                        as the slow give-

of-hot-flesh Takes,me;in crazier waves of light
sweetsmelling
                    fragrant:
                                    unspeakable chips
Hacked,
            from the immense sun(whose day is drooled
on night—)and the abrupt ship-of-her lips

disintegrates,with a coy!explosion

IV

first she like a piece of ill-oiled
machinery does a few naked tricks

next into unwhiteness,clumsily
lustful,plunges—covering the soiled
pillows with her violent hair
(eagerly then the huge greedily

Bed swallows easily our antics,
like smooth deep sweet ooze where
two guns lie,smile,grunting.)

"C'est la guerre"i probably suppose,
c'est la guerre busily hunting
for the valve which will stop this.
as i push aside roughly her nose

Hearing the large mouth mutter kiss pleece

V

The moon falls thru the autumn Behind prisons she grins,
where people by huge whistles scooped from sleep land breathless
on their two feet, and look at her between bars. She stands
greenly over the flat pasteboard hill with a little pink road
like a stand of spilled saw-dust. The sentinel who walks asle
ep under apple-trees yawns. The moon regards little whores
running down the prison yard into the dawn to shit, and she is
tickled too. (Trees in morning are like strengths of young
men poised to sprint.) There's another sentinel wanders al
ong besides a wall perhaps as old as he. The little moon
pinks into insignificance:a grouch of sun gobbles the east—
  She is a white shadow asleep in the reddishness of
Day.

VI

The moon-lit snow is falling like strange candy into the big eyes of the little people with smiling bodies and wooden feet

hard thick feet full of toes

left-handed kiss

I think Berthe is the snow,and comes down into all corners of the city with a smelling sound. The moon shines all green in the snow.

then saw I 1 Star cold in the nearness of sunset. the face of this star was a woman's and had worked hard.   the cheeks were high and hard, it powdered them in a little mirror before everybody saying always nothing at all   The lips were small and warped,it reddened them. Then one cried to it & it cried Je viens and went on looking at itself in the little mirror saying always nothing —Then I ask the crowding orange—how is that star called? she answers Berthe, changing into a violet very stealthily
O with whom I lay
Whose flesh is stallions
Then I knew my youth trampled with thy hooves of nakedness

23years lying with thee in the bed in the little street off the Faubourg Mon martre

   tongue's cold wad knocks

VII

Perhaps it was Myself sits down in this chair.   There were two
      chairs,in fact.
My fur-coat on.   Light one cigarette.   You
came her stalking straw-coloured body, cached with longness of
      kimona.
   Myself got up out of a chair(there are two)say "Berthe" or
something else. Her Nudity seats ltself sharply beside.   New
person. —The champagne is excellent sir.— so we are drinking a
little,and talked gradually of the war France death my prison,all
pleasant things.   "Je m'occuperai tout particulierement de vos
colis".   and send one to The Zulu,as i want, one to mon
camarade   "vous n'avez pas trop chaud avec la pelisse?"no...I
decline more champagne anyway "Vous partez—?demain
matin?""le train part a huit heures un quart"
   I watched her Flesh graciously destroy its cruel posture
"alors:il faut bien dormir
".then is to be noticed...plural darkness spanked with singular
      light over
the pink
bed
   To Undress—laughably mechanical   how my great ludicrous
      silent boots thrown off Eye each other,really
As she lay:the body a flapping rag of life;I see pale whim of
      suppressed face framed in the indignant hair,a jiggling
      rope of smile hung between painted cheeks. and the furry
      rug of tongue where her Few teeth dance slowly like
      bad women
                  My thumb smashes the world—
frot of furied eyes on brain!heart knotted with A suddenly nakedness—.

VIII

NOISE

thugs of clumsy mutter shove upward leaving fat
        feet-prints,rumbles poke buzzing thumbs
        in eye of world

stovelike emotion rapidly scrambles toots and
        scurry nibbling screams and sleek
        whistles which sprint ribbons of
        white shriek!   clatters limp,

from svelt blubbering tubes Big dins fuzzily
        lumber rub-bing their eyes

thin very chimney lips wallow gushing cubes
        of unhasty delirium,chunks of
        indolence waddle slowly.

bangs punch.

explosion after

explosion: from black lips sail chrome
        cries extra extra whatisit no?   Yes!
        no!   yea: extra wheel!   oh hear it
        what no-yes (extra! extra) who, said
        Yea?   what!   yea!   yes.

PEACE Joy's right boot squashes disciplined
        fragilities by slobber of,patient
        timidities undermined skyscrapers,
        Krash;it (explodes in a) plastic Meeow
        —with uncouth snarl of sculptural
        fur through which Claws

neatly

leap Wall Street wriggles choked with gesturing
        human swill squirms gagged with
        a sprouting filth of faces extra!
        PEACE millions like crabs about a

prosperous penis of bigness the woolworth
        building,slowly waving

factories-stores-houses-burstcrack—people!
        through,doorswindows,Tears a
        vomit of supernatural buttons

PEACE

biffing sky battles huge city which escapes
        niftily through slit-of-sunset
                          Broadway.
        dumb signs ripe

pustules of unhealth.   squEEzed:spatter
        pop-p-ings of mad

colour reveal,

canyons of superb nonsense.   Vistas of
        neatness bunged with a wagging
        humanity poised;In the bathing,

instant   a reek-of electric daintiness PEACE

all night from timetotime the city's accurate
        face peeks from smothering blanket
        of occult pandemonium

PEACE all night!   into dawn-dingy dimness:
        of almost

streets; capers a trickle of mucus
        shapes equals girls men.

a Woman
                of bronze
unhappy
                            stands
at the mouth
an oldish woman
                                    in a night-gown
                    Boosting a

torch
Always
            a tired woman
            she has had children
                                and They have forgotten
            Standing

                        looking out
to sea

X

hips lOOsest OOping shoulders blonde& pastoral hair,strong,
arms and smelling of HAY
woman in a carotcoloured skin yellow face chipsofanger splayed
from GriNDing-mouth waist pulledup on oneside SHOWED her
sweaty corset.
              eyeslike   smoky   idols

girl,iceblue hair huGe lips like orangepeels,waV ingagreat
tricolour
        yelling silently
                        cheery-nose square pash eyes splut
tering warench ofscarlet on right-breast legs
monumentally aPart
(Girl)flagstuck in her breasts. she bent her neck and bit It
jam mingIt deeper—pink—complexion tooth gone left side red
we epingeye s CHUBBY

their grey   hands tired of making   Death Probable

hairycheeks faces like hugestrawberries
                              they pass a funeral in
silence and their branches had a terrible greenness

                    La Grève the Goddess
                                  tooth less
witches from Whose.gumsBurs !tthe
                    Cry

leather faces,crinkling with Ideal,the common,people
let-out of darkNess

XI

this cigarette is extremely long,
i get them by the indigo box of 10.
And then, you were sitting across from me:
and my blood silkily telling i was, how wrong!
(i thinking to have remembered how
you were beautiful) this cigarette, when
inhaled, produces a mystery
like scented angels joking in a sharp soft row
(i buy 10 of them in an indigo box.)
Wrists. Elbows, Shoulders. Fingers.
the minute amorous stirs
of flesh invisibly visible (this
cigarette, exhaled in musical shocks
of kiss-coloured silence) by Christ kiss me.   One kiss

XII

love was—entire excellently steep

therefore(most deftly as tall dreams unleash
pale wish,between mirrors thoughts blundering
merge;softly thing forgets its name:
memories descending open—time reverses)
the million poets of our single flesh

gradually prepare to enter sleep

Around worldfully whom noises pour
carefully(exploding faintly)while(humbling

faintestly)among unminds go stumbling
cries bright whip-crash leaps lunge thundering
wheels and striving(are now faintestly)come
strutting such(wonderfully how through our

deepestly hearts immensely strolling)horses.

POEMS LEFT WITH ELAINE ORR
1918–1919

These poems were found among the possessions of Elaine Orr MacDermot, Cummings's first wife, after her death in 1975. Other poems in the group were "Epithalamion," the wedding song he had written for the marriage of Elaine and Scofield Thayer in 1916, and sixteen poems, mostly sonnets, that were published in *Tulips and Chimneys, &*, and *XLI Poems*. They were composed during and shortly after Cummings's term of service in the U.S. Army.

Since most of them were love poems, a little explanation seems needed. After an estrangement developed between Elaine and Scofield Thayer, Cummings fell in love with Elaine, and their love affair, which had begun even before Cummings was drafted into the army, continued in New York and Paris over the next three years. Elaine divorced Thayer and, after a long period of hesitation, married Cummings, but the new marriage lasted only a few months.

Cummings had sent this group of poems for Elaine to read, and although several of them, including "first she like a piece of ill-oiled," which has been placed in the previous section, "Reflections," described sexual experience with prostitutes, most of them were delicate love sonnets, such as "i have found what you are like" or "when you went away it was morning," that were later published in *XLI Poems*. Of the poems from this group now published here, the best one, "cherie / the very, picturesque, last Day," places their love on a legendary level with Paolo and Francesca, but also reveals, in a self-mocking way, Cummings's sense of guilt, while at the same time implying that he would willingly endure eternal damnation for Elaine's love.

let us suspect,chérie,this not very big
box completely mysterious,on whose shut
lid in large letters but neatly is
inscribed "Immortality".   And not
go too near it,however people brag
of the wonderful things inside
which are altogether too good to miss—
but we'll go by,together,giving it a wide
berth.   Silently.   Making our feet
think.   Holding our breath—
if we look at it we will want to touch it.
And we mustn't because(something tells me)
ever so very carefully if we
begin to handle it

        out jumps Jack Death

II

sometime,perhaps in Paris we will
have the enormous bright hour of evening
when lazily the prostitutes are taking
thither and hither their bright slender voices
along the boulevards,among the sitting
people in cafés
                    "the world is,you feel
(I just saw a man in a taxi who looked like God)
a little sudden whore skilfully dying
in Somebody's arms,on the way to the theatre."—"Did
you?"—"And just suppose it were.   Wouldn't poor Royce's
hair tremble?   What would Old Man Emerson
say?"—"Emerson would probably say 'I went to Paris
and found myself.'"—"Probably."—"And think of this one:
'Godal Mighty and Myself,by Frank Harris'!"

III

chérie
        the very,picturesque,last Day
(when all the clocks have lost their jobs and god
sits up quickly to judge the Big Sinners)
he will have something large and fluffy to say
to me.   All the pale grumbling wings

of his greater angels will cease:as that Curse

bounds neat-ly from the angry wad

of his forehead(then fiends with pitchforkthings
will catch and toss me lovingly to
and fro.)   Last,should you look,you
'll find me prone upon a greatest flame,

which seethes in a beautiful way
upward;with someone by the name
of Paolo passing the time of day.

IV

my little heart is so wonderfully sorry
lady,to have seen you on its threshold
smiling,to have experienced the glory

of your slender and bright going, and it is so cold
(nothing being able to comfort its grief)
without you,that it would like i guess to die.
Also my lady do i feel as if
perhaps the newly darkening texture of my
upon nothing a little clumsily closing
mind will keep always something who has

fallen,who being beautiful is gone
and suddenly.   As if you will point at the evening

"in this particular place,my lover,the moon
unspeakably slender and bright was"

V

the spring has been exquisite and the
summer may be beautiful.   But,
tell me with eyes quiteshut
did you love me,will you love me

and perfectly so forth;i see,
kissing you—only kissing
you(it is still spring
and summer may be beautiful)shall we

say years?   O let us say it,girl
to boy smiling while the moments kill
us gently and infinitely.

And believe(do not believe)there'll
be a time when even these leaves will

crawl expensively away.   My lady.

VI

willing pitifully to bewitch
the nude worm of my reaching mind,to tease
its gropings curiously i remark these
frivolous slowlywinking lives which
(like four or three pretty flies)the
very and tremulous architecture
of frail light suddenly will capture.
And i think
            (as if perhaps a tree
should remember how Spring touched it)of your
deep kiss which constructs faintly
in me an upward country(on whose new shores
the first day has not come,but it is quaintly
always morning and silence)always where

hang,in the morning,wistful corpses of stars.

VII

as
we lie side by side
my little breasts become two sharp delightful strutting towers and
i shove hotly the lovingness of my belly against you

your arms are
young;
your arms will convince me,in the complete silence speaking
upon my body
their ultimate slender language.

do not laugh at my thighs.

there is between my big legs a crisp city.
when you touch me
it is Spring in the city;the streets beautifully writhe,
it is for you;do not frighten them,
all the houses terribly tighten
upon your coming:
and they are glad
as you fill the streets of my city with children.

my love you are a bright mountain which feels.
you are a keen mountain and an eager island whose
lively slopes are based always in the me which is shrugging,which is
under you and around you and forever:i am the hugging sea.
O mountain you cannot escape me
your roots are anchored in my silence;therefore O mountain
skilfully murder my breasts,still and always

i will hug you solemnly into me.

VIII

my lady is an ivory garden,
who is filled with flowers.

under the silent and great blossom
of subtle colour which is her hair
her ear is a frail and mysterious flower
her nostrils
are timid and exquisite
flowers skilfully moving
with the least caress of breathing,her
eyes and her mouth are three flowers.   My lady

is an ivory garden
her shoulders are smooth and shining
flowers
beneath which are the sharp and new
flowers of her little breasts tilting upward with love
her hand is five flowers
upon her whitest belly there is a clever dreamshaped flower
and her wrists are the merest most wonderful flowers   my

lady is filled
with flowers
her feet are slenderest
each is five flowers her ankle
is a minute flower
my lady's knees are two flowers
Her thighs are huge and firm flowers of night
and perfectly between
them eagerly sleeping
is

the sudden flower of complete amazement

my lady who is filled with flowers
is an ivory garden.

And the moon is a young man

who i see regularly,about twilight,
enter the garden smiling to
himself.

IX

if you like my poems let them
walk in the evening,a little behind you

then people will say
"Along this road i saw a princess pass
on her way to meet her lover(it was
toward nightfall)with tall and ignorant servants."

POEMS FROM THE DIAL PAPERS
1919–1920

These poems come from a manuscript labeled "8 sonnets 16 other things," which was discovered by George Firmage in 1976 with pages of an incomplete copy of the earliest manuscript of *Tulips & Chimneys* that Cummings had given to Stewart Mitchell, the first managing editor of *The Dial*. The two manuscripts, catalogued merely as "Poems," are part of the Dial Collection in the Beinecke Library, Yale University. An accompanying note in Mitchell's hand, "Poems of E. E. Cummings / Given to me: June 1920 / RSM," evidently refers to "8 sonnets 16 other things." Four of the poems in this manuscript were later published in *Tulips and Chimneys, &, Is 5,* and *Viva;* the rest were forgotten until now.

Most of the seventeen pieces published here are love poems addressed to Elaine, but they differ from the earlier group by striving often for the expression of more complicated feelings. For example, in the poem "Above a between-the-acts prattling of" he attempts in his central metaphor to capture the mental activity that anticipates making love—and that may be an experience more subtly pleasurable than the consummation itself.

A few other poems are characteristic handlings of common Cummings motifs—an impression of the coming of dawn, a satiric rendering of religious preaching, a Dada-like presentation of the confusions of an urban scene in a snowfall. One piece, "my humorous ghost precisely will," is a personal poem reflecting some of Cummings's chief haunts in Boston and New York: the Old Howard Burlesque Theater; Minsky's National Winter Garden;

Hassan's Roumanian Hall, where Greek men enjoyed performing the handkerchief dance; Moskowitz's Roumanian Restaurant, where Cummings might see Jack Shargel, the top comedian at Minsky's; and finally Elaine's apartment at 3 Washington Square.

the comedian stands on a corner,the sky is
ve   ry   soF.   t   Ly.   Fal,   Ling   (snow

with a limousines the and whisk of swiftly taxis God

knows howmany mouths eyes bodies
fleetly going into nothing,

verysky the and.of all is,slow–
Ly.faLLing
                    ,f all in g)FaLlInG   odd
....which will. swiftly Hug   kiss   or

a drunken Man bangs silentl Y   into the moo
                                                                n
the comedian is standing.   On a corner   in-a-dream
of.(sn)ow,
                    in the nib; bling tune
OF
       "nextwehave the famous dancing team
swiftness & nothing
                              ,letergo
                                        Professor!

like most godhouses this particular house
of god utters a chilly smell....
Within,the rector's talking normal face
like a cat who plays with a dead mouse
skilfully mumbles about Hell,
pretending it's alive,knowing it is
not.   That head which(you'll confess)
looks like the apple whereby Adam fell
belongingly adorns the fat demure
hairless man sitting heavily with what
is obviously his wife,his small unthrilled
circular ears winking to the word of God
his large unclever mind carefully filled
with inexpensive christian funiture.

III

This is the vase,   Here

is the crisp and the only and the very sudden garden in
which the little princes strut,taller than
flowers

(here are,a thousand erect and bright
princes tenderly smiling and smiling forever)

this is the vase.
Here are a million alwaysmoving ladies
always moving,and moving slenderly
around a keen and little princess

taller than a day,

This
is the vase   here are a billion
warriors with furious and supple
faces like white nouns.   With
bodies like smiling and gigantic verbs

If we turn the
vase,slowly the little and
keen princess will come slender
-ly out of a million ladies.   The
bright and erect princes suddenly will strut
in the garden.   the soldiers
who are supple and who
are furious will become,
not only and crisply,
                              Gigantic and Smiling.
They will step from the
                          vase:

                          tearless,
                          together.
taller than Tomorrow

IV

my humorous ghost precisely will
stray from the others on the hill
if only to hear someone say
exactly what someone has said.

Straying as softly as a puma,
it will come to Boston
and sit in the Howard Atheneum
up under the non si fuma,

(up in the ceiling with the old men.
With the wrinkles and eyes and tumours.)
Precisely straying like a leopard
or a music,will my ghost

visit queerly the naked girls who
wiggle at the end of second avenue
in the Burlesque As You
Like it,or gliding most

softly into Hassan's will see
them all dancing together,a turk
and one girl and three greeks
with the cousin of the old Man In The Moon playing

the kanoon.   (After that,
precisely i will float into Moskowitz's
where there's himself at the zimbalon,and
Raisin tight with Jack Shargel at a table in the

spidery music,ordering Bosca
singing oona vaap and gesturing like a Petrouska.
And i'll gesture as well as i am able in the
transparent condition which ghosts

are afflicted with,
my gestures will be in the past tense
and bright and small and ridiculous.)
And after all i'll go to a certain

house where the window is open
i will go in between the curtains
silently,like a cat or a tune.   I will find
softly and precisely a particular room where

you are perfectly asleep in your hair,
and you will kiss my ghost thinking
that it's a dream,until i leap from you
suddenly out into the morning

V

dawn

and now.begins
f e e l i n g
roofs
a cool-
ness-Before-light,(hush
) it's the indescribable minute

(noises
happen
Bigly!   a milk-wagon
totters(by,its sleepy horses step-
ping like clockwork,a driver scarcely alive.)bAnGiNgLy
along which The little a street absurdly new
        :Houses
are,with firm
light   wonderful,but and

suddenly)

hear?do you birds begin which all to talk,loudly
in the disappearing air

VI

Above a between-the-acts prattling of
the orchestra conducted by memory and behind this
justfallen curtain of uneasy flesh
which is a girl

certain things shout and curse
turning on lights setting up walls amid
a very efficient confusion as certain
other things i dare say take their
proper places wiping their mouths adjusting a cravat and
settling one's vest or smoothing
the hair
and one immaculately tailored
thing inhales a cigarette un-
clenching and clench
-ing plump fingers
and peeping at the audience

Because these to me wholly i
confess impertinent
noises are better than the politeness of
silence or that is to say when the curtain
rises   and to all the other people who
are my multitudinous cleansmelling selves
who are sitting waiting to be thrilled

Illusion!

makes its rubber gesture,

decidedly i refuse my lady your beautifully
imbecile invitation to hasten the play

VII

when time delicately is sponging sum after
sum memory after memory
from the neatening blackness
of my mind

and i am not exactly old,

(but Spring is

Plunging in the big absurd world with
a difference)and when the mauled

flower of your mouth
is old and cold,and bold....

i think(excuse me if i
speak the truth)you will be yellow & sick
for me(your
mouth and the rest of you whatever
that is,i suppose

breasts and throat,legs and hands.)   Lady
in that
day i think
(it's only thinking.   Your pardon if i err.)
i think you will be tired of telling
me & my dreams to go to hell

VIII

sometimes i am alive because with
me her alert treelike body sleeps
which i will feel slowly sharpening
becoming distinct with love slowly,
who in my shoulder sinks sweetly teeth
until we shall attain the Springsmelling
intense large togethercoloured instant

the moment pleasantly frightful

when,her mouth suddenly rising,wholly
begins with mine fiercely to fool
(and from my thighs which shrug and pant
a murdering rain leapingly reaches the
upward singular deepest flower which she
carries in a gesture of her hips)

IX

o my wholly unwise and definite
lady of the wistful dollish hands

(whose nudity hurriedly extends
its final gesture lewd and exquisite,
with a certain agreeable and wee
decorum)o my wholly made for loving
lady
    (and what is left of me
your kissing breasts timidly complicate)

only always your kiss will grasp me quite.

Always only my arms completely press
through the hideous and bright night
your crazed and interesting nakedness

—from you always i only rise from something

slovenly beautiful gestureless

X

my youthful lady will have other lovers
yet none with hearts more motionless than i
when to my lust she pleasantly uncovers
the thrilling hunger of her possible body.

Noone can be whose arms more hugely cry
whose lips more singularly starve to press her—
noone shall ever do unto my lady
what my blood does,when i hold and kiss her

(or if sometime she nakedly invite
me all her nakedness deeply to win
her flesh is like all the 'cellos of night
against the morning's single violin)

more far a thing than ships or flowers tell us,
her kiss furiously me understands
like a bright forest of fleet and huge trees
—then what if she shall have an hundred fellows?

she will remember,as i think,my hands

(it were not well to be in this thing jealous.)
My youthful lust will have no further ladies.

XI

lady you have written me a letter
which i will never keep in a foolish vermilion
box glad with possible dragons

but in a surer place,and in a better
place and in a richer(and
if sometimes i will take it out,to see
how it is,perhaps you will understand
perhaps you will know that a million

things happen richly in me.)
And where i will put it away my lady
you will understand,only if once
(if leaning and with little breasts apart
you quickly will look into the

dark box of my shutting heart

XII

but   turning a corner   ,i
(Of)was am aware a talkative
huge.ness moo.vingOne(tree   a huge,talking   of rain;squabb
-ling leaves the.high   .a)
tree!Is or
(is it leaves)the   are.filled
with moving.the colour
of,night the is it col,our of the
isColoured   mobile&supreme
dark,
Ness.
colour of rain.
Ness. dark,ness.   colour of the.   colour Of of

i
am a therefore
little unsorry   for our
bodies,bodies of.you & me and
unsorry because you   and   me are is
one,tree   unsorry;that
(youandme,the)bodies!of,first singular
Am strong and moving & answerable to oblivion.

XIII

you said Is
there anything which
is dead or alive more beautiful
than my body,to have in your fingers
(trembling ever so little)?
                              Looking into
your eyes Nothing,i said,except the
air of spring smelling of never and forever.

....and through the lattice which moved as
if a hand is touched by a
hand(which
moved as though
fingers touch a girl's
breast,
lightly)
              Do you believe in always,the wind
said to the rain
I am too busy with
my flowers to believe,the rain answered

XIV

is
it

because there struts a distinct silver lady

(we being passionate O yes)upon
the carpet of evening which thrills
with the minuteness of her
walking,for she walks

upon the evening
                    shy and luxurious   .and because

we
being

passionate perceive o Yes where(immensely
near)
simply,

but with a colour like the ending of the world
rises

        slow
            ly

balloonlike

            the huge foetus of The Moon   ?

—with our gestures we pry
and our mouths battle into distinctness.   It
is this kiss which builds in us ever so softly

the coarse and terrible structure of the night.

XV

as one who(having written
late)sees his light
silenced.

              and going to his window
              a little while he
                              watches
              the inevitable city's

reborn enormous whisperless

                         Body
                         (and

sees
       over & between the roofs

                         the lifted streets
                         un-

                         speak.
                         -ing

                              and he does not
speak.)But perhaps
inhaling a possible.cigarette
he is sorry and
pitiful.and he quietly repeats to
himself
         something peculiar and small and dead

And goes to sleep miserable & tall.

                         —so,my
                         lady is
                              your lover

when he a little closes his eyes
thinking "tonight i did not lie in her bed." and the Light

The
tall
extraordinary   Light   ,It

goes rapidly over the perhaps world(over
the possible Now & the lilies.over

 Whoever & me?)

 nouns and

              violets   !

                    ships,   &   countries

XVI

in front of your house i

stopped for a second in the
rain,in the Spring.
At the window
              only your hands

              beautifully,
              were

(and the green bird perched carefully upon

                                    a gesture

knew me.)

XVII

Lady,i will touch you with my mind.
Touch you and touch and touch
until you give
me suddenly a smile,shyly obscene

(lady i will
touch you with my mind.)Touch
you,that is all,

lightly and you utterly will become
with infinite ease

the poem which i do not write.

POEMS FROM THE 1920s

Most of these poems, which were found scattered among a great many unfinished or discarded items in the Cummings Collection at Harvard, were written in the early years of the decade when Cummings was at work on the poems that later appeared in *Is 5*, and on his play, *Him*. In fact, "now two old ladies knitting" anticipates his use of the characters of the Norns who act as a chorus in *Him*.

From time to time, the style represents Cummings's attempt to duplicate the spirit of Cubism (especially in the first poem "the newly") or Dadaism. Some of the presentations of the Parisian streets, such as "taxis toot whirl people moving perhaps laugh into the slowly," seem closer to *assemblage*, that seemingly random patterning developed by the Dadaists, than they do to any literary style, even the improvisational declamations that Ezra Pound called *Cantos*.

The principal scenes are those of Cummings's years in Paris with his first wife, 1921–23, including the Champs-Elysées where he loved to see the children playing on the merry-go-round or watching the puppet show ("c'est Le Diable and. punch"), and the restaurant that now was his favorite, La Reine Blanche, across from the Cluny Museum. A few are set in New York; for instance, we are given a glimpse of the Syrian restaurant Khoury's, on Washington Street, where Cummings delighted in the baba gahnouj and stuffed vine leaves.

The attitudes come mostly from the early 1920s, too: first, the uninterrupted happiness with Elaine, later the troubles that beset their relationship, and finally the anguish that resulted from the divorce. One item included in this section, "this fear is no longer dear," is not really a poem, but a note from Cummings to Elaine. It can serve as an illustration of the way Cummings sometimes expressed himself in notes and letters to the women he loved—he would speak in the unusual diction and phrasing of his poems.

the newly

cued
motif smites truly to beautifully
retire through its english

the forwardflung backwardspinning top returns fasterishly
whipped the top leaps bounding upon other tops to caroming
off persist displacing its own and their lives who
grow slowly and first into different deaths

concentric arithmetics of transparency slightly
joggled sink through algebras of proud

inwardlyness to collide spirally with iron geometries
and mesh with
which when both

march outward into the freezing fire of thickness

everywhere is updownwardishly
found nowherecoloured curvecorners
gush silently into solids
more fluid than gas

now two old ladies sit peacefully knitting,
and their names are sometimes and always

"i can't understand what life could have seen in him" stitch
-counting always severely remarks;and her sister(suppress-
ing a yawn)counters "o i don't know;death's rather attractive"
—"attractive!why how can you say such a thing?when i think
of my poor dear husband"—"now don't be absurd:what i said was
'rather attractive',my dear;and you know very well that
never was very much more than attractive,never was

stunning"(a crash.   Both jump)"good
heavens!" always exclaims "what
was that?"—"well here comes your daughter"
soothes sometimes;at which

death's pretty young wife enters;wringing her hands,and wailing
"that terrible child!"—"what"(sometimes and always together
cry)"now?"—"my doll:my beautiful doll;the very
first doll you gave me,mother(when i could scarcely
walk)with the eyes that opened and shut(you remember:
don't you,auntie;we called her love)and i've treasured
her all these years,and today i went through a closet
looking for something;and opened a box,and there she
lay:and when he saw her,he begged me to let him
hold her;just once:and i told him 'mankind,be careful;
she's terribly fragile:don't break her,or mother'll be angry' "

and then(except for
the clicking of needles)there was silence

"out of the pants which cover me
frostbitten limbs from pole to pole
I thank whatever tailors be
for this unconquerable hole.
A little Porter tingaling
is pleasant even for Sweeney in the Spring."

And at these words a sullen murmur ran
out of the University of Pennsylvania.
"However which may be;
I grow old,I grow old,

I shall tell the tailor what he should be told."—
And as he spake Lars Porcelain
struck his bathtub
exclaiming,in words of one syllable,Eheu fugaces Postume.
(and nobody knew what daisy knew

for all men kill the thing they love:

Some does it with a turn of the screw....
and go wilde afterwards he adding settled
his frustrated celluloid collar.

pound pound pound
on thy cold grey corona oh P.

but I would that my tongue could utter
the silence of Alfred Noise.

Speak speak thou Fearful guest;tell me,immediate
child of Homer—when you wrote The Dial Cantos did you know
of the organ and the monkey?

Tears,idle Tears!   I know not what you mean....
dear little Sweeney,child of fate,
how dost thou?—And the stiff dishonoured nightingales:

fled is that music.   (I perceive
a with undubitably clotted hinderparts in obviously

compatriot;let us step into this metaphor.)

5.

2 shes

both not quite
young perfectly

respectable obviously married

women each a you
know soup son more
a(with of course their well
above their showing)

sit Sat LOOK

ing and lookanding andlookingand at
what That)then i
start
ed
laughing obvicouldn't

ouslyhelp itwhy be

cause the
he can you sitting
on that very bench in perfectly
bright obviously sunlight Right
before Every
one the yes Hole

WORLD was(praying chin up eyes

tightshut locked
hands pray)ing unbeliev
able he real
(was young was
niceyeslooking but some

Yes

how weak sort of or i doano)the
atrical now you
got me laughing but we shooden eye
can't helpid omygod hehehemygodhegodmy

god.   Allatonce the apparition

arose and
looking straightahead
offwalked

dis(

appea)ring a
mong treestreestrees

greennewlying

II

I.

When parsing warmths of dusk construe
The moon a noun of personal blood
Subject to that veteran verb
Of imperative vacancy

The velvet tiger of my soul
Washing in fundamental mind
Ellided chaos hating
Leases sensation absolute

Then clustering to the average green
Slants the huge ship of total lust
Footed with foam and clewed with stars
Into my gaunt uneating heart

2.

Lady,since your footstep
is more frail than everything
which lives,than everything which breathes
in the earth and in the sea
because your body is more new,

a dream(skilfully who mimics,entirely who pictures
yourself a skilfully and entirely moving dream
with fingers,a dream with lifted little breasts
and with feet)touches

me through the day scarcely,timidly;

whereas,beside me through the long night and upon
me,always i feel the crisply and deeply moving
you which is so glad to be alive—

the you with hot big inward stealing
thighs,perfectly who steal me;or as the wise

sea steals entirely and skilfully the ignorant earth.

being(just a little)
too tired from kissing
for thinking or anything
except dreaming,
let us suppose

O my lady:at dusk
between the earth and the sea

ourselves,you and i together mysteriously and always floating,

moving;absorbing mysteriously(or as desire absorbs
a dream)and(as if we were dream or dreams)mysteriously
engulfed by fatal immensities of twilight—O imagine(softly as
we,our minds,mysteriously together moving float always

between the ocean and the world)that,smiling,i remark to
you:of these five waves the wave

which waits is most great;

(of these nine roses,you
reply seriously,she who chiefly hides
herself is deepest)

Lady

i pray to what is unimaginable,
to your smile
which will not even allow even my pencil
nearer than a thousand miles.

i pray to your eyes
whose niceness decides my pen
it is a thick fool.

my brushes go big and stupid
and their colour(s)turns to paint before
your laughter,to which i kneel.

i worship at your tears
i approach your tears with my best chisels
(but in your least tear there is nothing
conceivable)
          my chisels stutter and wobble.

But chiefly i entreat your timidity
(i mean that aspect of you which so easily can
explore completely and enjoy the occult textures,
consult wholly and continually the invisible edges,of that and this:
distinguish swiftly and exquisitely

in all things what entirely is alive.)

III

THE RAIN IS A HANDSOME ANIMAL

Whereupon i seize a train and suddenly i am in Paris toward night,in Mai.
Along the river trees are letting go scarcely and silently wisps,parcels
of incense,which drop floatingly through a vista of talking moving people;
timidly which caress hats and shoulders,wrists and dresses;which unspeak-
ingly alight upon the laughter of men and children,girls and soldiers.
In twilight these ridiculous and exquisite things descendingly move among
the people,gently and imperishably.   People are not sorry to be alive.
People are not ashamed.   People smile,moving gaily and irrevocably moving
through twilight to The Gingerbread Fair.   I am alive,I go along too,I
slowly go up the vista among the hats and soldiers,among the smiles and
neckties,the kisses and old men,wrists and laughter.   We all together ir-
revocably are moving,are moving slowly and gaily moving.   Intricately the
shoulders of us and our hats timidly are touched by a million absurd hint-
ing things;by wisps and by women and by laughter and by forever:while,
upon our minds,fasten beautifully and close the warm tentacles of evening.

AFTER SEEING FRENCH FUNERAL

in front of the cathedral hovered a mumbling nobody:its greenish fumbling flesh swathed with crumbling alive rags,its trunk topped abruptly by a slouch hat under which carefully existed the deep filthy face and out of which sprouted wisely a decayed yellowish width of beard.

he came out just at noon:the little Place Saint Michel banged and tooted in shallow hard sunlight;from all which upreaching through white fog the boulevard hung,in a maze of sticky colour punched here and here at intervals by black blunt shapes or where some hobgoblin trees poking sprouted amputated hands.

taxis toot whirl people moving perhaps laugh into the slowly
millions and finally O it is spring since at all windows
microscopic birds sing fiercely two ragged men and a
filthiest woman busily are mending three wholly broken somehow
bowls or somethings by the web curb and carefully spring is
somehow skilfully everywhere mending smashed minds
O
the massacred gigantic world
again,into keen sunlight who lifts
glittering selfish new
limbs
and my heart stirs in his rags shaking from his armpits the
abundant lice of dreams laughing
rising sweetly out of the alive new mud my old
man heart striding shouts whimpers screams breathing into
his folded belly acres of sticky sunlight chatters bellows
swallowing globs of big life pricks wickedly his
mangled ears blinks into worlds of colour shrieking
O begins
       the mutilated huge earth
again,up through darkness leaping
who sprints weirdly from its deep prison
groaning with perception and suddenly in all filthy alert things
which jumps mightily out of death
muscular,stinking,erect,entirely born.

long ago,between a dream and a dream

(when monsieur matal directed la reine blanche
opposite cluny's gladly miraculous most
vierge et l'enfant)someone was morethanalive
with love;with love:with love—love of whom?
love:paris;la france,une fille and at least

(while every night was a day and a day was dimanche)
seven or—not to exaggerate—certainly five

selves beyond every human imagining my;
whereas,in this epoch of mindandsoul,to feel
you're not two billion other unselves is enough
to scare any no one nearly-if-not-quite stiff
—how did(i often ask me)that someone die?

but just as often the answer's only a smile

them which despair
do we despise,being seated
in the cave's oblong darkness
having commanded our minute glasses
of colourless fire.
Nothing is better than this
except which has not happened,thence
i bid you(as very deeply you near the gates of
Hell)cast like Euridyce one brief look behind
yourself.
        Voilà Monsieur Le Patron,
excuse me:I was talking.   He pours
quickly skilfully just.
It.   Glistens.

Voilà—the waterhued extract of Is

believe:sipping,enter my arms;let us invade sumptuously
the hurrying extravagant instant....come mon amie
let us investigate suddenly
our lives,let us drink calvados,

let us shut ourselves into the garret of Now
and swallow the key.

6.

Paris,thou art not
merely these streets trees silence
twilight,nor even this single star jotting
nothing busily upon the green edges of evening;
nor the faces which sit and drink on the boulevards,laughing
which converse smoke smile,thou art
not only a million little ladies fluttering merely upon darkness—

these things thou art and thou art all which is alert perishable
alive:thou art the sublimation of our
lives eyes voices
thou art the gesture by which we express to one another all
which we hold more dear and fragile than death,
thou art the dark dear fragile
gesture which we use

Life 's—let us not too much protest—not clumsy
more than another thing.   Nor ungainly
but(after all)of a convenient size:
not too minute to die about
nor too big to lie about.

softly above everything the strolling
upward ghost of le tour Eiffel quietly wonderfully
hangs;haunting the mai.

Perfectly a year,we watched Together les enfants jumping and
cry Prenez garde Monsieur c'est Le Diable and.punch jerk

bonnes giggled-background slope,Erect

...under grEEnoftrees;shadowily

  sof tness

                mon ami
                    hoary
goldfish pluc k ing
at bread
       2balloons   red&blue   tiedtogethergo Up.bumP ingand
HOpPinG

the merrygoround
               (eternal)
boats,
  leaping with wind comingin SatisFiedor st:uck under the
  central fountain

               and;spherical chestnut-trees
soldiers,Le Jardin

and(still)in the louvre the knight sleeps 8 monksbear Him with
bent?heads his feet rest,on his Dog

    paris
     paris
      paris
 it was about to rain and,a thousand girls came-marching into
the same garden flinging their marching Spurting youth
                            on the
grass

            green
        things branches in Their hands red on their Breasts crowns
    of fleur d'oranger on brown heads
    as if they had torn upthe World bytheroots
all seeking the sunlight-Bridegroom

                                    large mouth of Jean little

a young Place soldier chucks de la half a dozen of oranges
République uptothe sitters on the Monument
                                        the women cry
                                        vive le poilu

voilà deux sous
he's forced to take their money;

look
my fingers,which
touched you
and your warmth and crisp
littleness
—see?do not resemble my
fingers.   My wrists hands
which held carefully the soft silence
of you(and your body
smile eyes feet hands)
are different
from what they were.   My arms
in which all of you lay folded
quietly,like a
leaf or some flower
newly made by Spring
Herself,are not my
arms.   I do not recognise
as myself this which i find before
me in a mirror.   i do
not believe
i have ever seen these things;
someone whom you love
and who is slenderer
taller than
myself has entered and become such
lips as i use to talk with,
a new person is alive and
gestures with my
or it is perhaps you who
with my voice
are
playing.

when of your eyes one smile entirely brings down
the night in rain over the shy town of my mind
when upon my heart lives the loud alive darkness
and in my blood beating and beating with love
the chuckling big night puzzles asquirm with sound
when all my reaching towers and roofs are drenched with love
my streets whispering bulge my trembling houses yearn
my walls throb and writhe my spires curl with darkness

then in me hands light lamps against this darkness(hands here
and there hands go thither and hither in my town)

carefully close windows shut doors

this fear is no longer dear.   You are not going to America and
i but that doesn't in the least matter.   The big
fear Who had us deeply in his fist is
no longer,can you imagine it
i can't which doesn't matter
and what does is possibly this dear,that we
may resume impact with the inutile,collide
once more with the imagined,love,and eat sunlight(do
you believe it?   i begin to and that doesn't matter)which i
suggest teach us a new terror whereby shall always brighten
carefully those things we consider life

IV

I.

                    the other guineahen
died of a broken heart and we came to New York.
I used to sit at a table,drawing wings
with a pencil that kept breaking and i kept

remembering how your mind looked when it slept
for several years,to wake up asking why.
So then you turned into a photograph

of somebody who's trying not to laugh
at somebody who's trying not to cry

2.

love's absence is illusion,alias time

(a shadowy hell whose inmates war to seize
each nothing which all greedy wraiths proclaim
substance;all frenzied spectres,happiness)

lovers alone wear sunlight.   The whole truth

(not hid by matter;not by mind revealed)
which never was by any living death
or dying life(and never will be)told

sings only—and all lovers are the song.

Here(only here)is freedom;always here
no then of winter equals now of spring
but april's day transcends november's year

(eternity being so sans until,
twice i have lived forever in a smile)

Float

ing
ly)
  i
   (in Khoury's warm

ish
)look

ing at thousands of
winter afternoons,through a
sometimes
a window In khoury
's

womB

for Ladies and Gents
like Restaurant
(always in Whom faces)
o ra mi

(sleep tick
s clock and
occasionally upon the)

perdreamhapsing
(floor cats drift)

birds meet above the new Moon
an instant:drooping,describe suddenly
arcs of craziness;chasing each
other,disappear wisely into the texture of twilight....

She is as slender as an accident
and seems to notice nothing—
perhaps
what is worthy of her comprehension
does not exist
(or else

in her mute way this portion of a circumference
understands all mysteries)

—birds crying to each other
faintly whirl and
pivot in thickening air;now is the melted moment of terror and of
dreams but the earth rising imperceptibly merging with the
lost sea bends inward and
entirely,subtly vanishes.

tonight the moon is round golden entire.   It
is satisfied and fragile,it does not
ask questions

such as "do you earn your living?   And if
not why not" or "how,under the circumstances,will
you support yourself?"   The moon is
round,not interested in
conduct
yellow
and complete.   Before proceeding
anywhere she takes care to surround her keen and
punctual circumference with an opaque
nimbus of perfectly safe colour,having
done which the moon
strides patiently along the wide quiet sky

like an intense disinterested virgin.

Who(finding herself with child)is peculiarly
careful not to lose the luminous smile which
has broken more than a handful of hearts,sent
a good many bright eyes into the dirt
hurried several big words into worms:

O poor moon
you will have a morning,
but you will be eventually slender
and noone will know unless perhaps the blind
force who laughs behind the sky.

the profound clown,Spring

LATE POEMS
1930–1962

These poems, selected from a great many that Cummings kept by him for years, some unfinished, some awaiting further polish, some withheld for one reason or another, represent Cummings in his mature years and manner. Here we can see his linguistic play more fully developed and controlled than in earlier years—his scrambled word order in syntactic anagram, his extension of the semantic possibilities of words that he chooses to stretch, squeeze, or intensify by typographical acrobatics or grammatical innovations. Here more than elsewhere in this volume is the fullest evidence of his basic outlook on life: his valuing of vitality ("aliveness") whether it be vigor of wit or physical expression of the uniqueness of being, such as the insect described in the first poem, "this(a up green hugestness who and climbs)." Cummings's elegy for his friend Henry Allen Moe, head of the Guggenheim Foundation, contains his highest praise in the word "lively," even though Moe's ugliness of appearance is frankly described as "loathesome."

Likewise, his social attitudes are fully on display—his celebration of individualism and rejection of groupiness. As a New England follower of Emerson and Thoreau, he deplored the twentieth-century American tendency toward collective social action and the growing pressures for conformity. His little parable about "alf," who was shot dead for his refusal to join the "frankiegang," lay on his desk in 1962 the day that he himself met death, stricken by a brain hemorrhage.

In form and subject the poems are quite representative of the work that came from his typewriter in his last thirty years. There are several satires—from a good-natured jibe at Ezra Pound's literary debt to Joyce, to a sour observation on the blatant homosexual flirting that was common in Tunisia when he visited Hammamet, or a scornful comment on the decline of academic standards at Harvard after the war (the "late unpleasantness"). There are, as usual, a number of love poems, these now addressed to his third wife, Marion Morehouse, the beautiful fashion model he had met in 1931. There are erotic poems, including one, "n w," written when he was sixty-seven years old. A couple of rollicking songs, the final pair in part 2, were intended for a musical comedy he had in mind for a time in the 1950s—the one entitled, "I'm very fond of," was to be sung by a group of baggy-trousered tramps and nude chorines.

There is an increase in the number of nature poems that Cummings wrote in these later years as he came to treasure, more and more, the summers he spent in New Hampshire in his private Eden, Joy Farm. His special reverence for the natural life was heightened and intensified by his hostility toward science and technology. He felt that mechanism had ruined New York City and that the depths of evil had been plumbed when scientists produced the atomic bomb—and political and military leaders had used it to destroy two Japanese cities. Two poems, here, refer to that horror. (In the poem, "April" / this letter's dated / "23," we should identify Joe Gould: he was a Harvard graduate who lived in Greenwich Village as a homeless derelict supported by handouts from artists and writers who appreciated his wit; he was natural man surviving in the urban environment.)

Frequently associated with the nature poems in these years is a religiosity that began to grow in Cummings after the mid-1930s. It was a religious feeling characteristically Unitarian, arising from a sense of a transcendent Unity, the spirit of which pervaded the universe and was especially to be identified with the natural phenomena of the heavens, like the stars ("a seething fearfully infinitude of gladly glorying immortalities"), or with the life principle that developed vegetative life and carried it through the cycle of the seasons. This idea of deity or supreme otherness he refers to as "illimitable Mystery" in the ballade, "does something lie who'd rather stand." The diminutive "i," which Cummings had always used for the self that speaks in his poems, now becomes in the last poems of this volume even more humble than before, surrounded by a vast expanded universe that is kept in operation by a principle beyond mind.

|

I.

this(a up green hugestness who and climbs)

alive this crumb(infinitesimal
this chip of being)jump does twenty times
easily unitself
                    making my soul
wholly rejoice(and my only heart so full
of amazing god,each every bounce of blood
perfectly equals several trillion ams)

this(now rewandering one grassblade)how

occult particle of vitality did
totally transform the—and i mean
(sans blague)totally—universe with one
gesture.
                    Thanks,colossal acrobat!
stupendous artist,feeble i salute

spontaneous insuperable you

             cont)-
  in
     this
             crazily
  per
  c
    hedtown(screams a
  & screams
)&
  screams
  A
  n(about to
  bring for
                t)hW
  omb
  an
     -(in
  u,
  all;
  y:

mary green
cheerful & generous
flew to america
(just like a dream)

fearless & loyal
(honest & strong)
utterly irish
& realer than sunlight

it's lucky the man is
herself will make happy
(though poor he'll be rich &
if old he'll grow young)

lively and loathesome moe's respectably dead

via(the papers are prudent)a heartattack:
dead is the whiteeyed face of,absurdly stuck
to its perfumed piglike body,a shark;and gone

"thiz-iz-un a chuf-tran-zish n" he frequently said

(married a nice gal who'd slaved in a buttonhole fac
tory:did odd jobs;ran errands like crazy,read black
stone every night;and landed skyhigh)no down
and out poor sonofabitch could possibly fail

to get a dollar from moe("meye sel-veye-wuz poor")

but nobody doublecrossed him and lived.   Somehow
it's devilish hard to realize we won't any more
hear his "sew-lawn-gooi eyel bih-seen-gyoo"

which maybe
           (and Only A Just Judge knows)
                         he will

"think of it:not so long ago
this was a village"
                    "yes;i know"

"of human beings who prayed and sang:
or am i wrong?"
                    "no,you're not wrong"

"and worked like hell six days out of seven"
"to die as they lived:in the hope of heaven"

"didn't two roads meet here?"
                              "they did;
and over yonder a schoolhouse stood"

"do i remember a girl with blue-
sky eyes and sun-yellow hair?"
                              "do you?"

"absolutely"
            "that's very odd,
for i've never forgotten one frecklefaced lad"

"what could have happened to her and him?"
"maybe they waked and called it a dream"

"in this dream were there green and gold
meadows?"
            "through which a lazy brook strolled"

"wonder if clover still smells that way;
up in the mow"
                    "full of newmown hay"

"and the shadows and sounds and silences"

"yes,a barn could be a magical place"

"nothing's the same:is it"
                              "something still
remains,my friend;and always will"

"namely?"
              "if any woman knows,
one man in a million ought to guess"

"what of the dreams that never die?"
"turn to your left at the end of the sky"

"where are the girls whose breasts begin?"
"under the boys who fish with a pin"

6.

out of bigg

est the knownun
barn
's
on tiptoe darkne

ss

boyandgirl
come
into a s
unwor

ld 2 to

be blessed by
floating
are
shadows of ove

r us-you-me a

n
g
e
l

s

II

I.

the phonograph may(if it likes)be prophe
tic:for instance let me recount to you,in
Sapphics quite dissimilar unto A.Swin
burne's the adventure

of Our Ezra,delver in mines strictly aes
thetic(short aes long as it happens by ex
ception)subjects,per what is loosely called a
Victor Victrola

—then right doggishly cocking one ear(bowwow)
our hero heard suddenly His Master's Voice:
"O Ezra, dear Ezra,come home to us now
for the clock in the(yes)steeple strikes(Yes)Joyce"

2.

in hammamet did camping queers et al)
with caverns measureless to man and how
lest which your worships deem apocryphal
o get a load of yonder arab now

bowed by the gaze of pederasts he queens
upon his toe and minces at the sand
the sorrows of young werther in his teens
and in his pants the urging of the hand

near and more near their draping selves redrape
lascivious hips against insisting sky
can there be no asylum no escape?
(his donkey looks mohammed in the eye

bud(spiggy nuvduh fienus

cundry unduh fuggnwurl Who
Ray)this do

odling u
th with one muddy fu
t parked on yon polished readingru

mtable is a foo
llfledged soo
perstoo
dent of what was harvard yoo

niversity until a few
late unpleasantnesses made edew
cation trew

ly you
niversal by simply&silently substitou

ting for A(not C but)Bminus

April"
    this letter's dated
        "23,
1946" and if anything
could prove the unprovable coming of such a spring
as nobody every imagined(including me)

Joe(for it's he)Gould's final remark would more
than execute perform achieve and do
the socalled trick with a universe to spare
(a universe far from excluding you)

so let us now pay strict attention "Af
ter all our genial friend the atomic bomb
is merely the transmutation of metal dream
ed of by mediaeval alchemists."   Paragraph

(who sighed "a rose,By any other name
would smell as"?
          Juliet)
            "Hoping you're the same

come from his gal's
alf whistle song
meet frankiegang
"join us or else"
"what for i should"
alf drop like dead

gang grow&grow
grab all the dough
everyone give
who want to live
we small it strong
it right we wrong

so goodbye alf
you just a bum
go fug yoseself
because freedumb
means no one can
dare to be man

"she had that softness which is falsity"
he frowned "plus budding strictly chasms of
uninnocence for eyes:and slippery
a pseudomind,not quite which could believe

in anything except most far from so
itself(with deep roots hugging fear's sweet mud
she floated on a silly nonworld's how
precarious inexistence like some dead

provocatively person of a thing
mancurious and manicured)i gave
the wandering stem a vivid(being young)
yank;and then vanished.   Seeing which,you dove

and brought me to the surface' smiling "by
my dick,which since has served me handily"

says ol man no body—
datz woty say
yez,honey
But
we don't care an
we'll just sing:O
Sumpn
ter Sumpn an
lipster
lips ahmindy
OuterCo
ro
naofyohr
SolarE
clipse

I'm very fond of
black bean
soup(O i'm
very
fond of black
bean soup
Yes i'm very fond
of black bean soup)But
i don't disdain
a beef-
steak

Gimme gin&bitters to
open my
eyes(O gimme
gin&
bitters to open
my eyes
Yes gimme gin&bitters
to open my eyes)But
i'll take straight rum as
a night-
cap

Nothing like a blonde for
ruining the
blues(O nothing
like a
blonde for ruining
the blues
Yes nothing like a blonde
for ruining the blues)But
i use redheads for
the tooth-
ache

Parson says a sinner will
perish in the
flames(O parson
says a
sinner will perish
in the flames
Yes Parson says a sinner
will perish in the flames)But
i reckon that's better
than freez-
ing

Everybody's dying to be
someone
else(O every
body's
dying to be some
one else
Yes everybody's dying
to be someone else)But
i'll live my life if
it kills
me

devil crept in eden wood
(grope me wonderful grope me good)
and he saw two humans roaming
—hear that tree agroaning

woman chewed and man he chewed
(open beautiful open good)
and their eyes were wet and shining
—feel that snake aclimbing

lord he called and angel stood
(poke me darling o poke me good)
with a big thick sword all flaming
—o my god i'm coming

III

I.

love's the i guess most only verb that lives
(her tense beginning,and her mood unend)
from brightly which arise all adjectives
and all into whom darkly nouns descend

love is a guess
that deepens
(time is a rose
which opens)
                    your eyes,my
darling,are two
young worlds of dew

never yet named
a stillness
(wholly undreamed
what frailness)
                    not quite may
twilight's until
rival your smile

truer how much
than yearning
(newer to touch
than morning)
                    your life is
only like one
star after rain

we being not each other:without love
separate,smileless—only suppose your

spirit a certain reckoning demands...

wondering what ever is become of
with his acute gradual lusting glance
an illdressed wellmoving foolishwise

(tracking the beast Tomorrow by her spoor)
over the earth wandering hunter whom you
knew once?

        what if(only suppose)

mine should overhear and answer Who
with the useless flanks and cringing feet
is this(shivering blond naked very poor
indeed)person that in the first light

standing washes my nightmare from his eyes?

4.

skies may be blue;yes
(when gone are hail and sleet and snow)
but bluer than my darling's eyes,
spring skies are no

hearts may be true;yes
(by night or day in joy or woe)
but truer than your lover's is,
hearts do not grow

nows may be new;yes
(as new as april's first hello)
but new as this our thousandth kiss,
no now is so

she,straddling my lap,
hinges(wherewith I tongue each eager pap)
and,reaching down,by merely fingertips
the hungry Visitor steers to love's lips
Whom(justly as she now begins to sit,
almost by almost giving her sweet weight)
O,how those hot thighs juicily embrace!
and (instant by deep instant)as her face
watches,scarcely alive,that magic Feast
greedily disappearing least by least—
through what a dizzily palpitating host
(sharp inch by inch)swoons sternly my huge Guest!
until(quite when our touching bellies dream)
unvisibly love's furthest secrets rhyme.

6.

n w
O
h
S
LoW
h
myGODye
s s

b
et
wee
n no
w dis
appear
ing mou
ntains a
re drifti
ng christi
an how swee
tliest bell
s and we'l
l be you'
ll be i'
ll be ?
? ther
efore
let'
s k
is
s

8.

when
      (day's amazing murder with)
                        perhaps

those mountains turn into these dreams who are
becauselessly themselves;alive and steps

one if(precisely nowhere from)of star,

what more than mere most spaceless and untimed
actual perfectly existences
through me have you eternally and roamed

—but still our you and i resemble us!

being without attempt each miracle
more isful than believe,how should we try
(like fictional poor minds whom fact can fool)
to live so ludicrous as death a lie?

only some silence called a thrush dares sing
(ours is a truth so beautifully young)

there are so many tictoc
clocks everywhere telling people
what toctic time it is for
tictic instance five toc minutes toc
past six tic

Spring is not regulated and does
not get out of order nor do
its hands a little jerking move
over numbers slowly

                  we do not
wind it up it has no weights
springs wheels inside of
its slender self no indeed dear
nothing of the kind.

(So,when kiss Spring comes
we'll kiss each kiss other on kiss the kiss
lips because tic clocks toc don't make
a toctic difference
to kisskiss you and to
kiss me)

time,be kind;herself and i
know that you must have your way

have it gently with ma belle—

but for beauty,understand,
life(and also you)would end

—time,she's very beautiful

Us if therefore must forget ourselves)
or?if because more
than sleep like sleep are
they move who cannot be(never may

live have pain grow joy)alive
(therefore and or
if should night what open beyond all
memories a tomorrow of descending

brightful undeath)make
we why prayer for how things which do
not move and stern or with proudly
and peace

or only(and if because
we shall into silent go)into whitely
i shall?
go(into snow you will Go

12.

now winging selves sing sweetly,while ghosts(there
and here)of snow cringe;dazed an earth shakes sleep
out of her brightening mind:now everywhere
space tastes of the amazement which is hope

gone are those hugest hours of dark and cold
when blood and flesh to inexistence bow
(all that was doubtful's certain,timid's bold;
old's youthful and reluctant's eager now)

anywhere upward somethings yearn and stir
piercing a tangled wrack of wishless known:
nothing is like this keen(who breathes us)air
immortal with the fragrance of begin

winter is over—now(for me and you,
darling!)life's star prances the blinding blue

every one of the red roses opened
(each in wholly her own amazing way
just as nobody else could ever have happened)"
up light spirits of mr and mrs dey

"well you know you said it was for a lady's"
michael's eyebrows "birthday" climbing "so"
(up light mrs and mr dey their bodies)
"naturally we're glad for her and you"

naturally(i sing to myself)imagine
that;imagine generous,gay,alive,
human:imag(and past their flowers a pigeon
swoops alighting on chaos of 10th)ine brave

"she's" proudly "so"(rose adds)"beautiful" and
dante(too)knew why the stars go round

I.

ringed

with monstrous
a doomed
world's huge how

thunders are

(s
lowl
y

but certainly)crum

bl
i
ng

each more silent than each

remind
ers of this or
of that

once(who knows)maybe

fearless
him or
beautiful

possibly her

and
even lov
ing

est youme

2.

G
  ra
   D
    ua
lLy &

     as(through waiting simplicities of

space)arrived   is
& suddenly Come makingly

silent descend,ingly creative(The

every
-Where
the from no-
where)The(silvery yesclowns

tumble!are made per!form

Featherish-nows-of-whiS

p
  e
   r
)s

    N
   o

  W

ance)danc

-ing millions all
whispers are

blossoms of touc-
h
-able everywhere

Is
(leap who
flow dive
a-

light
&
O)
such made of
yes whiter

than wonders come
kissingly creatures
of dreaming how skilfulest
Floatingl

-y every-
thing perfectly shining
are(angels)and

a ar are ar a
-n-

d(d

4.

Cri
   C
k

et
in
-visible every
whereish;faint.ly shrill Most

(keen)
bell Of,shy a

spirit
:twisting
cry!ex
      transparent
                 or

-din-

arywish;quick-
liest universal whis

per(Wis
      p
        Like un

                 thing
)hearable

oar in a such tre

men
dous Sea
     who

our
s e l v e s be
ing,Call "

                t
I
M
e

    " SometimeS

5.

leastlessly

out
of this
more steep of
that most noisy muchful

colour

a(silent and
beginning)how
impossibly

fragrance

swims
is(who

the

little

who)floating a silently wanders
and very carefully smiling
how shyly to
herself moon-
childdoll

-dream

s(

these out of in
finite no
where,who;arrive s
trollingly

:alight whitely and.

)now
flakes:are;guests,of t
wi
ligh

t

7.

rainsweet

s
tillnes
s

&

farnearf
uling
a thrush

's

v
oi
c

e

life
    shuts &)opens the world
goes upward
            ,Spring every
where beginningly
.breathes(feels with men girls
trees lakes birds cities are bright
crisp which new)slowly most out of a more slovenly
of out most a of darkness

              rise
              things,
                  move. MOVE. my

"life" in-ward-and-un-der-neath Its
ideas glides:whistling;naked:
strides,among
the clean hugeness of wind(leaps
tumbles a
foal)struts,

(erect
slim—.)
Born

like a little bear twilight
climbs clumsily and beautifully the
ladder of the sky(a whipped and very little
bear who goes through his
tricks awkwardly and rapidly at
some fair,fearful of the cracking
whip)and
rungs of
cloud bend one by one under the hustling hairy
body of twilight
of
a little bear helplessly who wipes
his eyes with his
paw when the lash flicks his face,

gallops wincing

into his cage
                    & a pale single
star(the performance being
concluded)bows solemnly to you & me

V

Ballade

does something lie who'd rather stand;
but if which tries to try to,the
universe opens like a wound:
spreadeagling on this bowery
dump's filthy floor a former e.
g. gentleman?—not my hands pry
fiercely that stinker from his pee
(because the poor sonofabitch is i)

do blood and flesh which danced and grinned
and skin more black than white are we
climb,jumping;at thick this rope's end:
to become such an itlike he
as,through space turning like a key,
unlocks all horror with one why?—
not my face screams in idiot glee
(because the poor sonofabitch is i)

on august sixth,let me remind
you,nineteen fortyfive a.d.
did a greengrocer from the land
of freedom and democracy
hurl out of relativity
some hundred thousand souls?—not my
life loathes that soulless s.o.b.
(because the poor sonofabitch is i)

illimitable Mystery
whom worlds must always crucify—
thanks be to God that You are me
because the poor sonofabitch is i

2.

for him alone life's worse than worst
is better than a mere world's best
whose any twilight is his last
and every sunrise is his first

all stars are(and not one star only)love

—but if a day climbs from the mountain of
myself,each bird alive will sing for joy

in some no longer darkness who am i

should far this from mankind's unmysteries
all nothing knowing particle who's i

look up,into not something called the sky

but(wild with midnight's millionary is)
a seething fearfully infinitude
of gladly glorying immortalities;

illimitable each transcending proud

most mind's diminutive how deathly guess

thing no is(of
all things which are
who)so alive
quite as one star

kneeling whom to
(which disappear
will in a now)
i say my here

6.

should this fool die

let someone fond
of living lay

in his left hand

a flower whose

glory by no
mind ever was

taught how to grow

APPENDICES

1.

DEDICATED TO DEAR NANA CLARKE

When looking at that picture, all the past
Life of the sweet one cometh back to me;
And with emotion deep, I think when last
I saw her, in this world of vanity.

2.

As rooms are separated by a curtain,
So are our lives; yes, like those rooms; the first
One is our present life; the second is
Our life to come,—our better life in Heaven;
The separating curtain,—it is death.

3.

OUR FLAG

O flag of the nation! O Red,White and Blue!
O symbol of liberty,waving anew!
All through our lives may we reverence thee,
The nation's bright ensign for liberty!

Dear flag,thou art sacred in peace and in war,
Where many have died for the stripe and the star,
Where many have died that the slave may be free,
Have died for the nation and liberty!

Thou has seen the great battles,thou hast witnessed the strife
And the din of the conflicts,death struggling with life,
And thy bright,waving banner,the dying could see
Who had fought for the nation and liberty.

So whenever we meet thee,it matters not where;
Be thou waving at home or on battlement bare,
May we stop and salute thee,whenever we see
The nation's bright banner for liberty.

4.

GOD

Great, good, just, kind and loving God,
Oh! tell us how we can ever
Thank Thee enough for what Thou hast done!
For the bond that none can sever,
That binds us mortals close to Thee,
And gives us wisdom and eyes to see.

For it is Thou who gives us strength
To try to be like Thee.
And working, pushing toward the goal
Of purity;
We let our better nature shine
Illumined by Thy light divine.

5.

THE RIVER OF MIST

Stretching away to westward the great river lies quiet beneath me.
So still it lies, that it seems as if it had not yet awakened from the
delicious sleep brought on by the silence of night.   A little distance
from the shore a boat is moored on its glassy surface,—perfect to every
detail the reflection glimmers below it.   All is still and sombre and
wonderful, as dawn gives way to daylight and night to morning.

As I stand leaning over the rail of the old wooden bridge that spans
it, I give full play to my imagination, and gaze ahead into the morning
fog that rests above its polished surface.   And as I gaze, gaze into
the deep white mist, my thoughts turn from earth to heaven, from mankind
to my God.   Far away, beyond the limits of that stream that fades into
the atmosphere, I can see a great celestial river and a great celestial
land.   Ah!   How my fancy pictures it,—how vivid and how real it seems!
How plainly I can see the inestimable future!   And how I doubly worship
the Great Power that has created all this.   How wonderful and how mar-
vellous it all is!   How sweet is this unconscious dreaming of the soul!

A slight sound from the waking city brings me back to ugly reality.
I turn my head backward.   In an instant, all the beauteous castles of
the future which my imagination so vividly builded, vanish from my mind.
All is gone!   Gone in a moment!   And nothing is left me but this world
as I turn away from the wonderful river of mist.

I.

The world is very big, and we
Are very small and ignorant,
But, till our Father doth transplant,
Into the garden we forsee—
Fragrant upon a far off lee—
Each frail and quickly withered plant,
He doth to each a duty grant,
And He hath given one to me!

To all the work that doth relate
To aiding these my fellow men,
To peace, to nation, and to state,
To noblest thought & impulse, when
The impulse comes—I dedicate
This heart, this soul, this mind, this pen!

2.

A chilly,murky night;
The street lamps flicker low,
A hail-like,whispering rain
Beats 'gainst the streaked,bleak pane;
The sickly,ghostly glow
Of the blurred,blinking,wavering,flickering light
Shines on the muddy streets in sombre gleams
Like a wierd lamp post on a road of dreams.

A dreary,heavy darkness;
In quivering folds it creeps
Over the shrouded world;
The leaves are dry and curl'd,
The soul of summer sleeps
In a black pall where all the world lies markless,—
And shrouded 'neath that form whose clammy breath
Chills as it clasps,he sleeps the sleep of death.

Night,thou canst not dismay!
For when,on life's dark eve,
Like flowers past their bloom,
We tenant that grim tomb,
And all behind us leave,
Know that from its cold clutch into the Day
We walk,preserved,uninjured;—comprehend
No fear,no hell,no misery,no End!

3.

THE PASSING OF THE YEAR

The world outside is dark; my fire burns low;
All's quiet, save the ticking of the clock
And rustling of the ruddy coals, that flock
Together, hot and red, to gleam and glow.
The sad old year is near his overthrow,
And all the world is waiting for the shock
That frees the new year from his dungeon lock.—
So the tense earth lies waiting in her snow.

Old year, I grieve that we should part so soon,—
The coals burn dully in the wavering light;
All sounds of joy to me seem out of tune,—
The tying embers creep from red to white,
They die.   Clocks strike.   Up leaps the great, glad moon!
Out peal the bells!   Old year,—dear year,—good night!

4.

EARLY SUMMER SKETCH

The rain
Drips down
O'er fields
All green
With grain.

Earth's gown
Is seen
Clinging
To her
In folds
Bedraggled.

The grey
Sky yields
Great drops
Down-winging
O'er tops
Of fir
And wolds
Green-gay
With Summer,
The new-comer.

For sod
Has haggled
With sky.

The tears
Fall fast
On high.

Aghast
And Dazed

Earth stands,
And lifts
Her hands,
To see
The wrong
Which she
Has done.

The sun
Breaks out
And sears
The drifts
Of cloud
That float
Along.

The shroud
No longer
Low-lies.

The note
Of the song
Of the bird
Is heard.

The cloud
Is furled.

Earth cries
A shout
Of gladness.

O'er skies,
And trees,
And leaf,
And leas
Of bay
Breaks day.

5.

SUMMER SONG

I

Warm air throbbing with locust songs,
Warm clouds screening the heavens' blue rifts.
Warm sun shadowing over-head cloud drifts,
Warm sky straining, earth-tethered, at her cloud-thongs.

II

Far away
A thrushes' choir trills.
Far away
The murmur of a river's rills,
Drumming of the thunder fist,
Coming of the rain mist,—
Peeping,
Creeping,
Leaping,
Sweeping
O'er the weeping
Hot hills.

6.

If freckles were lovely, and day was night,
And measles were nice and a lie warn't a lie,
    Life would be delight,—
    But things couldn't go right
    For in such a sad plight
I wouldn't be *I*.

If earth was heaven, and now was hence,
And past was present, and false was true,
    There might be some sense
    But I'd be in suspense
    For on such a pretense
You wouldn't be *you*.

If fear was plucky, and globes were square,
And dirt was cleanly and tears were glee
    Things *would* seem fair,—
    Yet they'd all despair,
    For if here was there
We wouldn't be *we*.

7.

THE EAGLE

I

It was one of those clear,sharp,mistless days
    That summer and man delight in.
Never had Heaven seemed quite so high,
Never had earth seemed quite so green,
Never had world seemed quite so clean
      Or sky so nigh.
    And I heard the Deity's voice in
      The sun's warm rays,
    And the white cloud's intricate maze,
And the blue sky's beautiful sheen.

2

I looked to the heavens and saw him there,—
    A black speck downward drifting.
Nearer and nearer he steadily sailed,
Nearer and nearer he slid through space,
In an unending aerial race,
      This sailor who hailed
    From the Clime of the Clouds.—Ever shifting,
      On billows of air.
    And the blue sky seemed never so fair;
And the rest of the world kept pace.

3

On the white of his head the sun flashed bright;
    And he battled the wind with wide pinions,
Clearer and clearer the gale whistled loud,
Clearer and clearer he came into view,—
Bigger and blacker against the blue.

Then a dragon of cloud
Gathering all its minions
　　Rushed to the fight,
And swallowed him up at a bite;
And the sky lay empty clear through.

4

Long I watched.　And at last afar
　　Caught sight of a speck in the vastness;
Ever smaller,ever decreasing,
Ever drifting,drifting away
Into the endless realms of day;
　　Finally ceasing.
　　So into Heaven's vast fastness
　　　Vanished that bar
Of black,as a fluttering star
Goes out while still on its way.

5

So I lost him.　But I shall always see
　　In my mind
The warm,yellow sun,and the ether free;
The vista'd sky,and the white cloud trailing,
　　Trailing behind.—
And below the young earth's summer-green arbors,
And on high the eagle,—sailing,sailing
　　Into far skies and unknown harbors.

8.

THE BOY AND THE MAN

Once upon a time
        A boy looked to the sky
        Where big white clouds lay furled,
        And he muttered with a sigh,
        "O,would I were a man!—
        How commonplace this world!
        Would I could roam and roam,
        Where all is strange and new,
        Where there are deeds to do,
        And find a grand,new home
        Where new folks came and went"—
        Thus did the boy lament,
        Ending as he began,—
        "O,would I were a man!"

Once upon a time
        A man looked to the sky
        Where big,white clouds lay furled,
        And he cried with a sigh,
        "O,would I were a boy!—
        How dear was that old world,
        With the dear ones ever close,
        Afar from strange,new places
        Full of unknown,staring faces,
        Unfeeling,and morose.
        Give me my home,God-sent!"
        Thus did the man lament,
        Groaning,"Gone boyhood's joy!
        O,would I were a boy!"

9.

God, Thine the hand that doth extend
    The booby prize of failure, and
The victor's chaplet in the end.
    God, Thine the hand.

God, mine the power to die or live,
    To find the earth-fruit sweet or sour,
To take and keep, or take and give.
    God, mine the power.

God, keep me trying to win the prize;
    Pamper me not, though I be crying.
Though snickering worlds wink owlish eyes,
    God, keep me trying.

10.

God make me the poet of simplicity,
    Force,and clearness.   Help me to live
Ever up to ever higher standards.   Teach me to lay
    A strong,simple,big-rocked wall
    Firmly,the first of all,
And to fill in the fissures with the finer stones and clay
    Of alliteration,simile,metaphor.   Give
    Power to point out error in sorrow and in felicity.
Make me a truthful poet,ever true to the voice of my
                Call,
    Groping about in the blackest night
    For ever clearer,dearer light,
Sturdily standing firm and undismayed on a Pillar of
                Right,
    Working with heart,and soul,and a willing might,
Writing my highest Ideal large in whatsoever I write,
    Truthfully,loftily,chivalrously,and cheerfully ever,
                Fearfully,never.

II.

On souls robbed of their birth-right's better part,
Born only in one world, through life to see
This nether sphere alone—God's pity be;
Poor, purblind purchasers at life's high mart.
The Great Physician, lest the ravaged heart
Reveal itself in anguish, did decree
The Lord of Sense, Contempt, that he set free
The mangled spirit from its memory-smart.
So, deep in scorn for him of perfect sight,
The blinded soul remembereth not her scars.

——But who hath sudden felt his spirit beat,
Sped through the smoking dark with fear-shod feet,
Still hounded, haunted, hunted down the night
By all the crying beauty of the stars?

12.

DEATH'S CHIMNEYS

Within,a coldly echoing floor:a terror
Of narrow,naked walls,whitened and ghastly,
Through whose grim hollowness,faint and incessant,
Is heard a murmuring horror of fires communing.
What flesh and blood,what hands and face,what beauty
Shrivels beneath the touch of flames caressing—
Becomes obliterate in this awful furnace?
What life dwelt in this formless heap of ashes
Drawn forth,—the fires subdued,the furnace opened,—
To inhabit yon dead vault of icy marble,
Under the day,dwelling in its own darkness,
Under the world,shrouded in its own silence?
What eye shall read this shadowy inscription?
What hand upon this cold thing lay its cypress?
What lip shall touch the silent vase of ashes?
The body,the human body divine,burning.

Without,warm flood of universal sunshine;
And a white butterfly,hovering,soaring,ascending...

13.

AFTER-GLOW

Blue water, and behind,
Benevolent orange sky,
And gentle sheep that troop
From their huge fields of cloud,
Hurrying, headed all
Homeward across the heaven,
Unto the western folds,
Where stands upon a hill,
Calling with gentle voice,
One cheery shepherd-star.

Stand still, O Shepherd! I,
With many other feet
And many, many flocks
From all the purple earth,
And all the yellow heaven,
Am coming, hurrying home,
Lifting mine eyes to thee,
And listening for thy call
Across the fragrant fields,
Adown the quiet world.

Grey water, yellow sky;
Alas! my star is gone,—
Departed, over the hill.
And all the flocks that heard
Their shepherd's call, and I,
Pause, midway in the rich
And honeyed middle heaven,
Sniffing the luscious sweet;—
No star, no shepherd.   Shall
We lag in the middle way?

No.   On, ye flocks!   And I,
Who heard his call, and saw
His tender, starry face,—
Down the soft, padded mead,
O'er fair, alluring fields,
Along ambrosial lands,
Away into the sun,
Will follow, follow him,
And farther, farther on,
And up, up, over the hill!

I.

BOOK IV, ODE 7

Farewell,runaway snows!   For the meadow is green,and the tree stands
   Clad in her beautiful hair.
New life leavens the land!   The river,once where the lea stands,
   Hideth and huggeth his lair.
Beauty with shining limbs 'mid the Graces comes forth,and in glee stands,
   Ringed with the rythmical fair.

Hope not,mortal,to live forever,the year whispers lowly.
   Hope not,time murmurs,and flies.
Soft is the frozen sod to the Zephyr's sandal,as wholly
   Summer drives Spring from the skies,—
Dying when earth receives the fruits of Autumn,till slowly
   Forth Winter creeps,and she dies.

Yet what escapes from heaven,the fleet moons capture,retrieving;
   When through Death's dream we survey
Heroes and kings of old,in lands of infinite grieving,
   What are we?   Shadow and clay.
Say will rulers above us the fate tomorrow is weaving
   Add to the sum of today?

Hear me:whatever thou giv'st to thine own dear soul,shall not pleasure
   Hungering fingers of kin.
Once in the gloom,when the judge of Shades in pitiless measure
   Dooms thee to journey within,
Birth,nor eloquent speech,nor gift of piety's treasure
   Opens the portal of sin.

Never,goddess of chasteness,from night infernal thou freest
   One who for chastity fell.
Ever,hero of Athens,him who loved thee thou seest
   Writhe in the chainings of Hell.

2.

The fetters of winter are shattered,shattered,
And the limbs of the earth are free,—
Spring,and the breeze that loveth the lea!
And the old keels—gaping and tempest battered—
Men roll them down to the sea.

Lo,how the sweet new magic bewitcheth
The hind with his fire-side dream;
The ox in his byre stamps with desire;
No more on the meadows the white rime pitcheth
His tents of a wintry gleam.

The Graces are dancing by mountains and gorges,
Like blossoms white in the moon;
Love is their light through the spell-bound night.
Under the world in Hell's huge forges
Hammers gigantic croon.

Open thy door;death knocks,who careth
For palace and hut the same.
Why wilt thou plan with life but a span?
All feel the hand that never spareth,
The fingers that know not fame.

Tomorrow—who knows?—in her train may bring thee
The city of dim renown.
There is nought redeems from the House of Dreams—
Ne'er again shall the kind dice king thee,
Never be Pleasure thy crown.

3.

Ah, Postumus, fleet-footed are the years!
  And what is Piety's imploring glance
To Age and Death, the dauntless charioteers?

My friend, think not to buy deliverance
  With smoking centuries of hecatombs.
It shall not profit thine inheritance.

King of the City of Unnumbered Homes,
  Who doth the monster and the brute compel,
Where the blind darkness ever gropes and roams,

By that black, languorous stream that winds in Hell,
  Whereon the noble and the knave must face
A common passage—wither, who can tell!—

Great Pluto, Postumus, implores thy grace!....
  Silence....Didst think those eyes, which are two stars,
Would suffer for thy sake one tear's embrace?

Although thou locked thy portals unto Mars,
  Nor e'er bestrode,—uncurbed by bit or rein,
Old Hadria's white horses,—'scaped the scars

Of the sword-edged sirocco, 'tis in vain.
  Fate bids that journey to Cocytus' stream,
And Danaus' ill-famed race behold again,

And Sisyphus, damned unto toil supreme.
  Fate sunders wife and husband, wedded brass
And miser; all and each, as in a dream.

How treacherous the treasures we amass!
  One only hath remembrance of our care,
The hated cypress-tree.   And so we pass.

Riving an hundred locks, and laying bare
  In its ripe age rich Caecuban divine,
Purer than pontiffs quaff, a lordlier heir
  Shall paint the pavement with thy titled wine!

4.

Who chides the tears that weep so dear a head?
Sorrowful Muse,for whom the father wed
The voice of waters to a cithern string,
Teach thou my grief to sing.

Ye sisters,Right and Honor,and forsooth
Unshaken Loyalty,and naked Truth,
Quintillius the peerless ye shall weep,
Who sleeps unending sleep.

Vainly,poor Virgil,rise thy pious prayers
To heaven which took him from thee unawares;
His memory many a noble friend reveres,
Thine were the bitterest tears.

What tho' more sweet thy lyre than his of Thrace,
When listening trees joyed in the music's grace,
Would life reclaim the shade from the beyond,
Which,with his fearsome wand,

The Shepherd,harsh the doors of fate to keep,
Has gathered once unto his shadowy sheep?
'Tis hard:but when 'twere impious to rebel,
Less grows the load borne well.

5.

BOOK IV, ODE 6
(An Invocation to Apollo)

O,blessed of the gods,
Shield of the race of Rome,
Are Faith and Fame at odds?
Thy smile is Spring.—O,too long thou dost roam,
    From home.

As a fond mother stands,
Seeking with prayerful eyes
O'er sea and sinuous sands
Her long-departed son,for whom black skies
    Arise.

So doth this land of ours
Yearn for her mighty son;
All lapped in fruit and flow'rs,
While on her waves the pinioned vessels run,
    Nor shun

The pirate or his kin.
The hearths of faith are pure,
And tamed is spotted sin.
With Caesar safe,where shall the savage boor
    Endure?

The mother loves to trace
In baby eyes and brow
Gleams of the father's face.
What's war with Spain?　Who fears the Scythian now?
    O,thou,

Upon thy Roman hills
Salute the drowsy light,

And lead the vine,that fills
Thy bowls,to the chaste tree in wedlock rite.
    Requite

The Gods with prayer and wine,
And as her heroes-Greece,
So,Roman,rank divine
Thy Caesar,with a joy which shall increase,
    Nor cease.

                * * * * * *

To thee the poet drinks—
"Long life!"—ere day is done;
"Peace to thy land!"—when sinks
Under the ocean,mellow eve begun,
    The sun.

UNCOLLECTED POEMS

Note on the Text

The thirty-six Uncollected Poems were originally published between 1910, when Cummings was sixteen years old, and 1962, the year of the poet's death. Until the publication, in 1991, of *Complete Poems 1904–1962*, they were available only in a variety of periodicals, a privately printed anthology of work by Cummings and his Harvard classmates, a volume of translations by the poet's friend D. Jon Grossman, and a book of photographs by Cummings's wife, Marion Morehouse, to which he contributed the text.

Uncollected Poems includes the poet's translation of Louis Aragon's *Le Front Rouge* with the French original *en face*. According to Cummings's account of his visit to the Soviet Union (*Eimi*, 1933), the translation was undertaken at the request of the Russian Revolutionary Literature Bureau as "a friendly gesture of farewell." The translator was quick to point out that Aragon's political beliefs were not his own; but "The Red Front" was not without interest as a poem, and its author and Cummings had been friends during the 1920s in Paris. Most important, the translation is excellent and one of the few mature examples we have of this phase of E. E. Cummings's art.

The texts and typography of the Uncollected Poems are based entirely on the original published versions, which are cited after each of the poems.

GEORGE JAMES FIRMAGE

I

TO WILLIAM F. BRADBURY

Leader and teacher, we whom you have taught,
Knowing that nothing ever can repay
The friendly aid that marked your honored stay,
Arise to thank and bless you. Where we sought
For help in that with which we could do naught,
You were at hand, prepared to show the way,
And when we came to you in sore dismay
You made most clear the path with perils fraught.

Now when we find ourselves about to lose
Your leadership, whose strength will ever dwell
In us and by us to the very end,
We know no better title we can use
In wishing you a final, fond farewell,
Than that which fits you best,—our faithful friend!

From *The Cambridge Review*, February 1910.

2

THE COMING OF MAY
Ballade

We have wintered the death of the old, cold year,
We have left our tracks in the melting snow,
We have braved harsh March's biting jeer,
And April's gusty overflow.
And now, when Nature begins to grow,
And the buds are out, and the birds are gay
And all is well—above and below,—
Here's to the coming of blithesome May.

Winter was good when he met us here,
With his sharp, clear days, and his flashing snow,
But we carried Winter out on his bier,
And buried him, many a month ago.
March was not hard with all his blow,
With April, Spring seemed on her way,
But we've reached the best at last, and so
Here's to the coming of blithesome May.

Winter has ended his cold career,—
No more death, and no more woe,—
We've come at last to a different sphere,
With no more freezing, and—mistletoe.
Spring in coming was very slow,—
Altogether too much delay,—
But we've cheered her on from foe to foe:
Here's to the coming of blithesome May.

Envoi

Think of the gratitude all must owe,—
Heaven has visited earth to-day.—
All the earth's in a warm, glad glow.—
Here's to the coming of blithesome May!

From *The Cambridge Review*, May 1910.

3

BALLAD OF THE SCHOLAR'S LAMENT

When I have struggled through three hundred years
    Of Roman history, and hastened o'er
Some French play—(though I have my private fears
    Of flunking sorely when I take the floor
In class),—when I have steeped my soul in gore
    And Greek, and figured over half a ream
With Algebra, which I do (not) adore,
    How shall I manage to compose a theme?

It's well enough to talk of poor and peers,
    And munch the golden apples' shiny core,
And lay a lot of heroes on their biers;—
    While the great Alec, knocking down a score,
Takes out his handkerchief, boohoo-ing, "More!"—
    But harshly I awaken from my dream,
To find a new,—er,—privilege,—in store:
    How shall I manage to compose a theme?

After I've swallowed prophecies of seers,
    And trailed Aeneas from the Trojan shore,
Learned how Achilles, after many jeers,
    On piggy Agamemnon got to sore,
And heard how Hercules, Esq., tore
    Around, and swept and dusted with a stream,
There's one last duty,—let's not call it bore,—
    How shall I manage to compose a theme?

Envoi

Of what avail is all my mighty lore?
    I beat my breast, I tear my hair, I scream:
"Behold, I have a Herculean chore.
    How shall I manage to compose a theme?"

From *The Cambridge Review* [October 1910].

4

SKATING

Spring is past, and Summer's past,
  Autumn's come, and going;
Weather seems as though at last
  We might get some snowing.
Spring was good, and Summer better,
  But the best of all is waiting,—
Madame Winter—don't forget her.—
    O
        You
           Skating!

Spring we welcomed when we met,
  Summer was a blessing;
Autumn points to school, but yet
  Let's be acquiescing.
Spring had many precious pleasures;
  Winter's on a different rating;
She has greater, richer treasures,—
    O
        You
           Skating!

Gleam of ice, and glint of steel,
  Jolly, snappy weather;
Glide on ice and joy of zeal,
  All, alone, together.
Fickle Spring!   Who can imprint her?—
  Faithless while she's captivating;
Here's to trusty Madame Winter.—
    O
        You
           Skating!

From *The Cambridge Review*, December [1910].

5

METAMORPHOSIS

We've plodded through a weird and weary time,
  Called Winter by the calendar alone;
We have beheld an earth pool-deep in slime,
  Image a heaven of stone.

We've found life hid between the folds of mire,
  Sensed life in every place, heard life in tune.
The earth-shell cracks with underneath desire;
  Spring crawls from the cocoon.

Her puny wings vibrant with will to grow,
  She clings, expanding like an opening eye;
More large, more able, more developed, lo,
  The perfect butterfly.

From *The Cambridge Review*, March [1911].

VISION

The dim deep of a yellow evening slides
Across the green, and mingles with the elms.
A faint beam totters feebly in the west,
Trembles, and all the earth is wild with light,
Stumbles, and all the world is in the dark.

The huge black sleep above;—lo, two white stars.

Harvard, your shadow-walls, and ghost-toned tower,
Dim, ancient-moulded, vague, and faint, and far,
Is gone!   And through the flesh I see the soul:
Colouring iron in red leaping flame,
The thunder-strokes of mighty, sweating men,
Furious hammers clashing fierce and high,—
And in a corner of the smithy coiled,
Black, brutal, massive-linked, the toil-wrought chain
Which is to bind God's right hand to the world.

From *The Harvard Monthly*, November 1911.

7

MIST

Earth is become the seat of a new sea;
Above our heads the splendid surges roll,
Only each mountain, like a steadfast soul,
Up through the strangling billows towers free.
Huge finny forms of phosphorescence flee—
Weird shadows—through the deeps, or caracole
With the sea-horses on some eye-less shoal,
Quickening the leafage of a wave-tombed tree.
As a great miser, morbid with his gain,
Pricked by unhealthy frettings, drowns dismay
In gorging on his plunders, one by one,—
Sudden—out of the vault of Heaven, the Sun
Unlocks the rainbow's glory, and the day.
The air is strange with rare birds after rain.

From *The Harvard Monthly*, February 1913.

8

WATER-LILIES

Behold—a mere like a madonna's head
Black-locked, enchapleted with lilies white;
By Him the Prince of Artists in Earth's sight,
Eons ere her most ancient master wed
With Immortality.   Such lustre, spread
So livingly before our starting sight,
Cries in the accents of its primal might:
"This artist and his art were never dead!"
See, when Dawn paints still water with the skies,
The wreath of consecrated faces rise,
With parted lips in fragrancy of prayer;
Look, while the ripening Night bends Heaven's bough,
Upon the mere—each spiritual brow
Sleeps in the floating halo of its hair.

From *The Harvard Monthly*, February 1913.

9

MUSIC

Music is sweet from the thrush's throat!
    Oh little thrush
    With the holy note,
Like a footstep of God in a sick-room's hush
    My soul you crush.

Unstopped organ, from earth you break
    To knock at the skies,
    And I can but shake
My fragile fetters, and with you rise
    Into Paradise.

But Love, your music requires not wings.
    To the common breed
    It clings, and sings:
"Heaven on earth is Heaven indeed.
    This is my creed."

From *The Harvard Monthly*, March 1913.

SUMMER SILENCE
(Spenserian Stanza)

Eruptive lightnings flutter to and fro
Above the heights of immemorial hills;
Thirst-stricken air, dumb-throated, in its woe
Limply down-sagging, its limp body spills
Upon the earth.   A panting silence fills
The empty vault of Night with shimmering bars
Of sullen silver, where the lake distils
Its misered bounty.—Hark!   No whisper mars
The utter silence of the untranslated stars.

From *The Harvard Advocate,* March 7, 1913.

I I

SUNSET

Great carnal mountains crouching in the cloud
That marrieth the young earth with a ring,
Yet still its thought builds heavenward, whence spring
Wee villages of vapor, sunset-proud.—
And to the meanest door hastes one pure-browed
White-fingered star, and little, childish thing,
The busy needle of her light to bring,
And stitch, and stitch, upon the dead day's shroud.
Poises the sun upon his west, a spark
Superlative,—and dives beneath the world;
From the day's fillets Night shakes out her locks;
List!   One pure trembling drop of cadence purled—
"Summer!"—a meek thrush whispers to the dark.
Hark! the cold ripple sneering on the rocks!

From *The Harvard Advocate,* March 21, 1913.

12

BALLADE

The white night roared with a huge north-wind,
And he sat before his thundering flame,
    Quaffing holly-crowned wine.
"Say me, who is she, and whence came
The snow-white maid with the hair of Inde?
    For I will have her mine!"

"She was crouched in snow by the threshold, lord,
And we took her in (for the storm is loud),
    But who, we may not know.
For, poorly-clad, she is strangely proud,
And will not sit at the servants' board,
    But saith she comes of the snow."

"She shall sit by me," he sware amain;
"Go, ere another ash-stick chars,
    Ask of her whom she loves."
"We ask her, lord, and she saith, 'The stars.'"
And he sware, "I will kiss with kisses twain
    Those cheeks which are two white doves."

The wind had tucked in bed her earth,
And tiptoed over valley and hill,
    Humming a slumber-croon;
And all the shining night lay still,
And the rude trees dropped their hollow mirth;
    Silently came the moon.

He rose from the table, red with wine;
He put one hand against the wall,
    Swaying as he did stand;
Three steps took he in the breathless hall,
Said, "You shall love me, for you are mine."
    And touched her with his hand.

White stretched the north-land, white the south...
She was gone like a spark from the ash that chars;
    And "After her!" he sware...
They found the maid.   And her eyes were stars,
A starry smile was upon her mouth,
    And the snow-flowers in her hair.

From *The Harvard Advocate*, April 25, 1913.

SONNET

A rain-drop on the eyelids of the earth,
That wakes the clod in flowers, and the skies
In depthless sunlight, and that mortifies
The soul, and drives it far from home and hearth
To seek the music of the Naiad's mirth
That laughs in falling waters, or surprise
The green tree—spirits with their dreaming eyes,—
The rosy baby of the May hath birth.

Delicious dark the hive of heaven drips;
Now in the firmament all shining crowd
The trembling, yearning stars, that cannot speak
For perfect joy; now steals a shadowy cloud,
A radiant tear, across the moon's pale cheek.
Dumbly the glorious sky yields up her lips.

From *The Harvard Monthly*, May 1913.

14

SONNET

Long since, the flicker brushed with shameless wing
The pale earth crucified, and to all lands
Bore the death-cry; uplifting her frail hands,
You aged maple, bowed with sorrowing,
Caught the red life.   New skies new seasons bring.
Wee red men build their lodge of yellow sands
In the primeval grass; the willow stands
Donned in her ermine, to be crowned with Spring.

How high the sky's vast purple palace towers!
And lo, the pride of majesty beguiled,
With playful hands, King Winter's laughing child,
Sweet April Heaven, from that royal brow
Hath plucked the snowy wreath of cloud, and now
Flings from her lap the million fluttering flowers.

From *The Harvard Monthly*, May 1913.

Do you remember when the fluttering dusk,
Beating the west with faint wild wings, through space
Sank, with Night's arrow in her heart?   The face
Of heaven clouded with the Day's red doom
Was veiled in silent darkness, and the musk
Of summer's glorious rose breathed in the gloom.

Then from the world's harsh voice and glittering eyes,
The awful rant and roar of men and things,
Forth fared we into Silence.   The strong wings
Of Nature shut us from the common crowd;
On high, the stars like sleeping butterflies
Hung from the great grey drowsy flowers of cloud.

From *The Harvard Monthly*, June 1913.

NOCTURNE

When the lithe moonlight silently
Leaped like a satyr to the grass,
Filling the night with nakedness,
All silently I loved my love
   In gardens of white ivory.

Three fragrant trees which guard the gates,
Three perfume-trees which sweeten nights,
Rise upon heaven, full of stars
And dripping with white radiance.
   Her body is more white than trees.

Five founts of Bacchus, honey-cold,
Five showers making drunk the lawns,
Spout up a dark delicious rain
Filling the earth with sleep and tears.
   Her tresses are more sweet than wine.

Seven flowers which breathe divinity,
Seven wondering blossoms of embrace,
Open their glory to the moon,
Kissing white immortality.
   Her mouth is chaster than a flower.

When the fleet moonlight silently
Fled like a white nymph down the grass,
Leaving the night to loneliness,
All songfully I loved my love
   In gardens of white ivory.

The strings are silver to my harp,
And all the frame is ebony

I think the moon is blossoming—
My hungry fingers bite the strings—
   My harp becomes a flower, and blooms.

The strings are golden to my harp,
And all the frame is as a rose.
I think the moon is quivering—
My longing fingers search the chords—
   My harp becomes a heart, and breaks.

When the first day-beam silently
Broke like an arrow from the east,
Quivering unto the heights of dawn,
All silently I left my love
   In gardens of white ivory.

There are three trees which stand like dreams
Before the gates of ivory;
The moon has withered in the west—
My harp has withered—Hail the day!
   (Wherefore this dagger at my thighs.)

There are five founts which play like sleep
Upon the gates of ivory;
The moon is songless in the west—
My harp is songless—Hail the day!
   (Wherefore this dagger at my hands.)

There are seven flowers which smile like death
Within the gates of ivory;
The moon is broken in the west—
My harp is broken—Hail the day!
   (Wherefore this dagger at my heart.)

From *The Harvard Monthly*, March 1914.

17

SONNET

For that I have forgot the world these days,
To enter at the smokeless lodge, and take
Life naked at primeval hands, to make
Clean comrades of large things in mighty ways;
That I have wrestled with the huge dismays
Which make the high head bow, the strong heart quake,
That I have battled for a golden stake,
Richer by every terror and amaze,—

For that I have forgot the world her cries
In the vast painted silences, that men
Have meant me nothing, under the great skies,
Over the high hills of God's caress,—
Ye pitying elements!—be with me when
I kiss the little feet of foolishness.

From *The Harvard Monthly*, May 1914.

NIGHT

Night, with sunset hauntings;
A red cloud under the moon.
Here will I meet my love
Beneath hushed trees.

Over the silver meadows
Of flower-folded grass,
Shall come unto me
Her feet like arrows of moonlight.

Under the magic forest
Mute with shadow,
I will utterly greet
The blown star of her face.

By white waters
Sheathed in rippling silence,
Shall I behold her hands
Hurting the dark with lilies.

Hush thee to worship, soul!
Now is thy movement of love.
Night; and a red cloud
Under the moon.

From *The Harvard Monthly,* November 1914.

SONNET

No sunset, but a grey, great, struggling sky
Full of strong silence.   In green cloisters throng
Shy nuns of evening, telling beads of song.
Swallows, like winged prayers, soar steadily by,
Hallowing twilight.   From the faint and high,
Night waves her misting censers, and along
The world, the singing rises into strong,
Pure peace.   Now earth and heaven twain raptures die.

I knew your presence in the twilight mist,
In the world-filling darkness, in the rain
That spoke in whispers,—for the world was kissed
And laid in sleep.—These wild, sweet, perfect things
Are little miracles your memory sings,
Till heart on heart makes us one music again.

From *The Harvard Monthly*, Christmas 1914.

LONGING

I miss you in the dawn, of gradual flowering lights
And prayer-pale stars that pass the drowsing-incensed hymns,
When early earth through all her greenly-sleeping limbs
Puts on the exquisite gold day.   The Christlike sun
Moves to his resurrection in rejoicing heights,
And priestly hills partake of morning one by one.

I look for you when comes the beautiful blue moon,
When earth is as a queen whose soul hath taken flight,
Embalmed in the entire strength of perfect light.
The immense heaven, a vase of utter silence, towers
Vastward, beyond where dreams the unawakened moon,
Holding infinity and her invisible flowers.

The hours drum up to sunset; now the west awakes
To armies.   Suddenly across the firmament
Couriers of light spur forth their captain's high intent.
Now devout legions, mustering heavenward without cease,
Face the hushed hordes of night.   A trumpet-radiance breaks—
I see the young ranked glories marching down to peace.

Twilight, and great with silence of beginning dreams,
Yet haunted still by broken hosts in brave retreat,
Of blameless cohorts whelmed into sublime defeat,
Which, darkly under world their ragged spears withdraw,
Shall rise to fire the night in far victorious gleams,
When over the towered east leaps the white sword of dawn.

So do I want you, when in heavenly spaces God
Slips His white wonders on the silent trail of time;
When out the smoking eve begins to slowly climb
A great, red, fearsome flower, about whose fatal face

The faint moths gather and die—till withered pale, she nod
Far in the west, and morn the little dreams shall chase.

Now is the world at peace; Heaven unto her heart
Holdeth sublimities afar from touch of day,
Presents divine the fates shall never take away,
Unfaded memories, immortal ponderings,
The little knock of prayer whereby are thrown apart
Those inner doors which lead into all priceless things.

O night, mother divine of poetry and stars!
O thou whose patient face is nearest unto God,
Thou of chaste feet with beautiful oblivion shod,
Having the dear, swift-winged dark within thy hands,—
The prison invisible of souls thy peace unbars,
And love and I rise up into unspoken lands.

From *The Harvard Monthly*, April 1915.

BALLAD OF LOVE

Where is my love! I cried.
Life, I bid thee to say.
Who hath taken away
Her who sate at my side.
For whiter is she than any pearl;
But the nights be lonely and dread.
Life, what hast thou done with thy loveliest girl?
    Look to the wood, She said.
For the white bird, O, the white bird,
Sleep he toucheth the white bird,
The white bird and the red.

Give me her eyes! I cried.
For I would kiss them asleep,
That are so cool and deep,
So soft and wondering wide.
Bluer are they than ponds of dream;
But the skies be grey o'erhead.
Life, where may the eyes of thy fairest gleam?
    Look to the field, She said.
For the blue flower, O, the blue flower,
Night he stilleth the blue flower,
The blue flower and the red.

O, for her hair! I cried.
Her young and wonderful hair,
To hide my sorrow there,
In the heart of a shining tide.
For her hair is more yellow than Heaven's dawn;
But the world's last leaves be shed.

Life, where is thy youngest angel gone?
　　Look to the west, She said.
For the yellow light, O, the yellow light,
Death he moweth the yellow light,
The yellow light and the red.

From *The Harvard Monthly*, May 1915.

22

Not for the naked make I this my prayer,
That up and down the streets of life do go,
Having, save rags, no pleasant thing to wear,
Albeit the timid ways have put on snow
Against such wind as only God can blow:
Well 'ware art Thou that these have no redress,
For always in Thine eyes is all distress
Of bodies that without due raiment be;
But are there Souls in winter garmentless,
Be with them, God! and pity also me.

Not for the hungry has my spirit care,
Whether their bodies shall be filled or no,
With whom the world her bounty will not share,
Wherefore they move on feeble feet and slow,
Feeling dear Death within their bodies grow:
Thou knowest these at pain beyond confess,
For sorrow never may Thy ears transgress,
Though lips be locked and pain shall hold the key;
But are there Souls whom hunger doth oppress.
Be with them, God! and pity also me.

Not for the homeless do I ask, where e'er
The lights of Hell their haunting faces show,
The legion undesired anywhere,
Whose hearts Love shall not build in,—who shall sow
And reap such loneliness as murder's woe:
Thy gracious mouth to these shall acquiesce,
Which is so very wonderful to bless
The plundered heart with joy held long in fee;
But are there Souls that know not Love's caress,
Be with them God! and pity also me.

Envoi

Father, for this we thank Thee without cesse:
Death is the body's birthright, as I guess,
But are there Souls that walk in hopelessness,
Be with them God! and pity also me.

From *The Harvard Monthly*, July 1915.

23

SAPPHICS

When my life his pillar has raised to heaven,
When my soul has bleeded and builded wonders,
When my love of earth has begot fair poems,
    Let me not linger.

Ere my day be troubled of coming darkness,
While the huge whole sky is elate with glory,
Let me rise, and making my salutation,
    Stride into sunset.

From *The Harvard Monthly*, January 1916.

24

SONNET

I dreamed I was among the conquerors,
Among those shadows, wonderfully tall,
Which splendidly inhabit the hymned hall
Whereof is "Fame" writ on its glorious doors.
Cloaked in green thunder are the sudden shores
Guarding the lintel's gold, whence of the wall
Leaps the white echo; and within, the fall
Is heard of the eternal feet of wars.

Here, at high ease, saw I those purple lords,
Sipping the wine of unforgetfulness,
Upon thrones intimate with all the skies:
Roland, and Richard, 'mid the shining press;
Leonidas, belted with living swords;
And Albert, with the lions in his eyes.

From *The Harvard Monthly*, March 1916.

HOKKU

I care not greatly
Should the world remember me
In some tomorrow.

There is a journey,
And who is for the long road
Loves not to linger.

For him the night calls,
Out of the dawn and sunset
Who has made poems.

From *The Harvard Monthly*, April 1916.

BELGIUM

Oh thou that liftest up thy hands in prayer,
Robed in the sudden ruin of glad homes,
And trampled fields which from green dreaming woke
To bring forth ruin and the fruit of death,
Thou pitiful, we turn our hearts to thee.

Oh thou that mournest thy heroic dead
Fallen in youth and promise gloriously,
In the deep meadows of their motherland
Turning the silver blossoms into gold,
The valor of thy children comfort thee.

Oh thou that bowest thy ecstatic face,
Thy perfect sorrows are the world's to keep!
Wherefore unto thy knees come we with prayer,
Mother heroic, mother glorious,
Beholding in thy eyes immortal tears.

From *The New York Evening Post,* May 20, 1916.

27

W.H.W., JR.*
In Memory of "A House of Pomegranates"

Speak to me friend! Or is the world so wide
That souls may easily forget their speech,
And the strong love that binds us each to each
Who have stood together watching God's white tide
Pouring, and those bright shapes of dreams which ride
Through darkness; we who have walked the silent beach
Strown with strange wonders out of ocean's reach
Which the next flood in her great heart shall hide?

Do not forget me, though the sands should fall,
And many things be swept away in deep,
And a new vision uttered to the shore,—
If after days bespeak me not at all,
Nor other's praise awake my song from sleep,
Nor Poetry remember, anymore.

From *The Harvard Monthly,* June 1916.
*In a flattering joke, Cummings called his friend Scofield Thayer "Willard Huntington Wright, Jr.," in reference to his being a devotee of Wright, the author of *Modern Painting* and other writings on modern art.

28

FINIS

Over silent waters
                      day descending
                                       night ascending
floods the gentle glory of the sunset
In a golden greeting
                          splendidly to westward
as pale twilight
                  trem-
                      bles
                            into
                                  Darkness
comes the last light's gracious exhortation
                                          Lifting up to peace
so when life shall falter
                          standing on the shores of the
eternal
god
      May i behold my sunset
Flooding
                over silent waters

From *Eight Harvard Poets*, New York 1917.

29

because
an obstreperous grin minutely floats
out of this onelegged flower—
girl's eyes and
bounding timorously
caroms against quickly taxis

or a chiselled god's
Mother hugs carefully against her
stone dull little breast the
with rain streaked Boy,quietly whose
mutilated eyes remember flowers

these clouds
imitate curiously
a 1st judgment lightening
on top of the large bold soft noisy

world
        filling me promptly
        up:
in order that i may be sharply
emptied into Silence(which is

nothing;but whom we call,darkness)

From *The Little Review*, Spring 1923.

if(you are i why certainly

the hour softly is
in all;places which move
seriously

Together.

let)us fold wholly ourselves smil-
ing because we love,
as doomed few alert(flowers and

excellently upon whom Night
wanders and wanders and)wanders
Or since,in air

like bubbles Faces
occur(shyly

to
one by bright
brief
one be)punc

-tured:the,green
nameless caterpillar of evening nib,ble,s
Solemnly a whitish leaf of sky.

From *Broom*, January 1924.

Louis Aragon

FRONT ROUGE

Une douceur pour mon chien
Un doigt de champagne Bien Madame
Nous sommes chez Maxim's l'an mille
Neuf cent trente
On met des tapis sous les bouteilles
Pour que leur cul d'aristocrate
ne se heurte pas aux difficultés de la vie
des tapis pour cacher la terre
des tapis pour éteindre
le bruit de la semelle des chaussures des garçons
Les boissons se prennent avec des pailles
qu'on tire d'un petit habit de précaution
Délicatesse
Il y a des fume-cigarettes entre la cigarette et l'homme
des silencieux aux voitures
des escaliers de service pour ceux
qui portent les paquets
et du papier de soie autour des paquets
et du papier autour du papier de soie
du papier tant qu'on veut cela ne coûte
rien le papier ni le papier de soie ni les pailles
ni le champagne ou si peu
ni le cendrier réclame ni le buvard
réclame ni le calendrier
réclame ni les lumières
réclame ni les images sur les murs
réclame ni les fourrures sur Madame
réclame réclame les cure-dents
réclame l'éventail et réclame le vent
rien ne coûte rien et pour rien
des serviteurs vivants vous tendent dans la rue des prospectus
Prenez c'est gratis

31

A gentleness for my dog
A finger of Champagne Very well Madame
We are at Maxim's A.D. one thousand
nine hundred thirty
Carpets have been put under the bottles
so that their aristocratic arses
may not collide with life's difficulties
there are carpets to hide the earth
there are carpets to extinguish
the noise of the soles of the waiters' shoes
Drinks are sipped through straws
which you pull out of a little safety-dress
Delicacy
There are cigaretteholders between cigarette and man
there are silent people at the cars
there are service-stairs for those
who carry packages
and there's tissue paper around the packages
and there's paper around the tissue paper
there's all the paper you want that doesn't cost
anything paper nor tissue paper nor straws
nor champagne or so little
nor the advertisement-ashtray, nor the
advertisement-blotter nor the
advertisement-calendar nor the
advertisement-lights nor the
advertisement-pictures on the walls nor the
advertisement-furs on Madame the
advertisement-toothpicks the advertisement-fan and the advertisement wind
nothing costs anything and for nothing
real live servitors, tender you prospectuses in the street
Take it, it's free

le prospectus et la main qui le tend
Ne fermez pas la porte
le Blount s'en chargera Tendresse
Jusqu'aux escaliers qui savent monter seuls
dans les grands magasins
Les journées sont de feutre
les hommes de brouillard Monde ouaté
sans heurt
Vous n'êtes pas fous Des haricots Mon chien
n'a pas encore eu la maladie
O pendulettes pendulettes
avez-vous assex fait rêver les fiancés sur les grands boulevards
et le lit Louis XVI avec un an de crédit
Dans les cimetières les gens de ce pays si bien huilé
se tiennent avec la décence du marbre
leurs petites maisons ressemblent
à des dessus de cheminée

Combien coûtent les chrysanthèmes cette année

Fleurs aux morts fleurs aux grandes artistes
L'argent se dépense aussi pour l'idéal
Et puis les bonnes œuvres font traîner des robes noires
dans des escaliers je ne vous dis que ca
La princesse est vraiment trop bonne
Pour la reconnaissance qu'on vous en a
A peine s'ils vous remercient
C'est l'exemple des bolchéviques
Malheureuse Russie
L'U. R. S. S.
L'U. R. S. S. ou comme ils disent S. S. S. R.
S. S. comment est-ce S. S.
S. S. R. S. S. R. S. S. S. R. oh ma chère
Pensez donc S. S. S. R.
Vous avez vu
les grèves du Nord

the prospectus and the hand which tenders it
Don't close the door
the Blount will take care of that Tenderness
Up to the very stairs which know how to ascend by themselves
in the department stores
Days are made of felt
Men are made of fog The world is padded
without collision
You aren't crazy Some beans My dog
hasn't been sick yet
O little clocks little clocks
have you given enough dreams to the lovers on the great boulevards
and the Louis XVI bed with a year's credit
In the cemeteries the people of this so-well-oiled country
hold themselves with the decency of the marble
Their little houses resemble
chimneypots

How much are chrysanthemums this year

Flowers for the dead flowers for the great artistes
Money is also spent for ideals
And besides good deeds wear long black trailing gowns
on the stairs I only tell you that
The princess is really too kind
for the gratitude which is owed you
Scarcely if they thank you
It's the bolsheviks' example
Unhappy Russia
The URSS
The URSS or as they say SSSR
SS how is it SS
SSR SSR SSR oh my dear
just think SSSR
You have seen
the strikes in the North

Je connais Berck et Paris-plage
Mais non les grèves SSSR
SSSR SSSR SSSR

Quand les hommes descendaient des faubourgs
et que Place de la République
le flot noir se formait comme un poing qui se ferme
les boutiques portaient leurs volets à leurs yeux
pour ne pas voir passer l'éclair
Je me souviens du premier mai mil neuf cent sept
quand régnait la terreur dans les salons dorés
On avait interdit aux enfants d'aller à l'école
dans cette banlieue occidentale où ne parvenait qu'affaibli
l'écho lointain de la colère
Je me souviens de la manifestation Ferrer
quand sur l'ambassade espagnole s'écrasa
la fleur d'encre de l'infamie
Paris il n'y a pas si longtemps
que tu as vu le cortège fait à Jaurés
et le torrent Sacco-Vanzetti
Paris tes carrefours frémissent encore de toutes leurs narines
Tes pavés sont toujours prêts à jaillir en l'air
Tes arbres à barrer la route aux soldats
Retourne-toi grand corps appelé
Belleville
Ohé Belleville et toi Saint-Denis
où les rois sont prisonniers des rouges
Ivry Javel et Malakoff
Appelle-les tous avec leurs outils
les enfants galopeurs apportant les nouvelles
les femmes aux chignons alourdis les hommes
qui sortent de leur travail comme d'un cauchemar
le pied encore chancelant mais les yeux clairs
Il y a toujours des armuriers dans la ville
des autos aux portes des bourgeois
Pliez les réverbères comme des fétus de paille
faites valser les kiosques les bancs les fontaines Wallace
Descendez les flics

I know Berck and Paris-plage
But not the strikes in the SSSR
SSSR SSSR SSSR

When men came down from the suburbs
and at the Place de la République
the black wave formed like a shutting fist
the shops wore their shutters over their eyes
so as not to see the lightning pass
I remember the first of May nine hundred seven
when terror reigned in the gilded drawingrooms
The children had been forbidden to go to school
in that occidental district which was reached by only a feeble
distant echo of wrath
I remember the Ferrer manifestation
when on the Spanish embassy was crushed
the ink-flower of infamy
Paris not so long ago
thou hast seen the procession made for Jaurés
and the Sacco-Vanzetti torrent
Paris thy crossroads shudder still with all their nostrils
Thy pavements are always ready to leap in air
Thy trees to bar the way to soldiers
Turn back great body called
Belleville
Ohé Belleville and thou Saint-Denis
where the kings are prisoners of the reds
Ivry Javel and Malakoff
Call them all with their tools
the errandboys bringing news
the women with their heavy chignons the men
who come out of their work as if out of a nightmare
their feet still tottering but their eyes clear
There are always gunsmiths in the city
and autos at the bourgeois' doors
Fold the reflectors like wisps of straw
make the kiosks benches Wallace fountains waltz
Bring down the cops

camarades
Descendez les flics
Plus loin plus loin vers l'ouest où dorment
Les enfants riches et les putains de previère classe
Dépasse la Madeleine Prolétariat
que ta fureur balaye l'Elysée
Tu as bien droit au bois de Boulogne en semaine
Un jour tu feras sauter l'arc de Triomphe
Prolétariat connais ta force
Connais ta force et déchaîne-la
Il prépare son jour Sachez mieux voir
Entendez cette rumeur qui vient des prisons
Il attend son jour attend son heure
sa minute la seconde
où le coup porté sera mortel
et la balle à ce point sûre que tous les médecins social-fascistes
penchés sur le corps de la victime
auront beau promener leurs doigts chercheurs sous la chemise de dentelles
ausculter avec des appareils de précision son cœur déjà pourrissant
ils ne trouveront pas le remède habituel
et tomberont aux mains des émeutiers qui les colleront au mur
Feu sur Léon Blum
Feu sur Boncour Frossard Déat
Feu sur les ours savants de la social-démocratie
Feu Feu j'entends passer
la mort qui se jette sur Garchery Feu vous dis-je
Sous la conduite du Parti communiste
SFIC
vous attendez le doigt sur la gâchette
Feu
mais Lénine
le Lénine du juste moment
De Clairvaux s'élève une voix que rien n'arrête
C'est le journal parlé
la chanson du mur
la vérité révolutionnaire en marche
Salut à Marty le glorieux mutin de la Mer Noire
Il sera livré encore ce symbole inutilement enfermé

250

Comrades
Bring down the cops
On on toward the west where sleep
rich children and first-class tarts
Go beyond the Madeleine, Proletariat
let thy fury sweep the Elysée
Thou hast good right to the bois de Boulogne on weekdays
Some day thou wilt blow up the Arc de Triomphe
Proletariat know thy force
Know thy force and unchain it
It prepares its day Know how to see better
Hear that rumour which comes from prisons
It prepares its day it awaits its hour
its minute its second
when the mortal blow shall be struck
and the bullet so sure that all the social-fascist doctors
bent over the victim's body
will have a time making their searching fingers wander under the lace-chemise
sounding with instruments of precision its already rotting heart
They won't find the usual remedy
and will fall into the hands of the rioters who will glue them to the wall
Fire on Léon Blum
Fire on Boncour Frossard Déat
Fire on the trained bears of the social-democracy
Fire Fire I hear pass by
the death which throws itself on Garchery Fire I tell you
Under the guidance of the Communist Party
SFIC
you are waiting finger on trigger
Fire
but Lenin
the Lenin of the right moment
From Clairvaux rises a voice which nothing stops
It's the talking-newspaper
the song of the wall
the revolutionary truth on the march
Hail to Marty the glorious mutineer of the Black Sea
He shall yet be free that symbol in vain imprisoned

Yen-Bay
Quel est ce vocable qui rappelle qu'on ne bâillonne
pas un peuple qu'on ne le
mâte pas avec le sabre courbe du bourreau
Yen-Bay
A vous frères jaunes ce serment
Pour chaque goutte de votre vie
Coulera le sang d'un Varenne

Ecoutez le cri des Syriens tués à coups de fléchettes
par les aviateurs de la Troisième République
Entendez les hurlements des Marocains morts
sans qu'on ait mentionné leur âge ni leur sexe

Ceux qui attendent les dents serrées
d'exercer enfin leur vengeance
sifflent un air qui en dit long
un air un air UR
SS un air joyeux comme le fer SS
SR un air brûlant c'est l'es-
pérance c'est l'air SSSR c'est la chanson c'est la chanson d'octobre aux
fruits éclatants
Sifflez sifflez SSSR SSSR la patience
n'aura qu'un temps SSSR SSSR SSSR

Dans les plâtras croûlants
parmi les fleurs fanées des décorations anciennes
les derniers napperons et les dernières étagères
soulignent la vie étrange des bibelots
Le ver de la bourgeoisie
essaye en vain de joindre ses tronçons épars
Ici convulsivement agonise une classe
les souvenirs de famille s'en vont en lambeaux
Mettez votre talon sur ces vipères qui se réveillent
Secouez ces maisons que les petites cuillères
En tombent avec les punaises la poussière les vieillards
qu'il est doux qu'il est doux le gémissement qui sort des ruines.

Yen-Bay
What is this word which reminds us that a people can't be
gagged, that it can't be
subdued with the curving sword of the executioner
Yen-Bay
To you yellow brothers this pledge
For every drop of your life
shall flow the blood of a Varenne

Listen to the cry of the Syrians killed with darts
by the aviators of the third Republic
Hear the groans of the dead Moroccans
who died without a mention of their age or sex

Those who await with shut teeth
to practise at last their vengeance
whistle a tune which carries far
a tune a tune UR
SS a joyous tune like iron SS
SR a burning tune it's
hope it's the SSSR tune it's the song
it's the song of October with bursting fruit
whistle whistle SSSR SSSR patience
won't wait forever SSSR SSSR SSSR

In crumbling plaster
among the faded flowers of old decorations
the last clothes and the last whatnots
underline the strange survival of knick-knacks
The worm of the bourgeoisie
vainly tries to join its scattered fragments
Here a class convulsively agonizes
family memories disappear in fragments
Put your heel on these vipers which are awaking
Shake the houses so that the teaspoons
will fall out of them with the bedbugs the dust the old men
How sweet how sweet is the groan which comes out of the ruins.

J'assiste à l'écrasement d'un monde hors d'usage
J'assiste avec enivrement au pilonnage des bourgeois
Y a-t-il jamais eu plus belle chasse que l'on donne
à cette vermine qui se tapit dans tous les recoins des villes
Je chante la comination violente du Prolétariat sur la bourgeoisie
pour l'anéantissement de cette bourgeoisie
pour l'anéantissement total de cette bourgeoisie

Le plus beau monument qu'on puisse élever sur une place
la plus surprenante de toutes les statues
la colonne la plus audacieuse et la plus fine
l'arche qui se compare au prisme même de la pluie
ne valent pas l'amas splendide et chaotique
Essayez pour voir
qu'on produit aisément avec une église et de la dynamite

La pioche fait une trouée au cœur des docilités anciennes
les écroulements sont des chansons où tournent des soleils
Hommes et murs d'autrefois tombent frappés de la même foudre
L'éclat des fusillades ajoute au paysage
une gaieté jusqu'alors inconnue
Ce sont des ingénieurs des médecins qu'on exécute
Mort à ceux qui mettent en danger les conquêtes d'octobre
Mort aux saboteurs du Plan Quinquennal

A vous Jeunesses Communistes
Balayez les débris humains où s'attarde
l'araignée incantatoire du signe de croix
Volontaires de la construction socialiste
Chassez devant vous jadis comme un chien dangereux

Dressez-vous contre vox mères
Abandonnez la nuit la peste et la famille
Vous tenez dans vos mains un enfant rieur
un enfant comme on n'en a jamais vu
Il sait avant de parler toutes les chansons de la nouvelle vie
Il va vous échapper courir il rit déjà

I am a witness to the crushing of a world out of date
I am a witness drunkenly to the stampingout of the bourgeois
Was there ever a finer chase than the chase we give
to that vermin which flattens itself in every nook of the cities
I sing the violent domination of the bourgeoisie by the proletariat
for the annihilation of the bourgeoisie
for the total annihilation of that bourgeoisie

The fairest monument which can be erected
the most astonishing of all statues
the finest and most audacious column
the arch which is like the very prism of the rain
are not worth the splendid and chaotic heap
which is easily produced with a church and some dynamite
Try it and see

The pickaxe makes a hole in the heart of ancient docilities
crumblings are songs wherein suns revolve
Men and walls of yesterday fall struck with the same thunder bolt
The bursting of gunfire adds to the landscape
a hitherto unknown gaiety
Those are engineers, doctors that are being executed
Death to those who endanger the conquest of October
Death to the traitors to the Fiveyearplan

To you Young Communists
Sweep out the human debris where lingers
the magical spider of the sign of the cross
Volunteers for socialist construction
Chase the old days before you like a dangerous dog

Stand up against your mothers
Abandon night pestilence and the family
You hold in your hands a laughing child
a child such as has never been seen
He knows before he can talk all the songs of the new life
He will get away from you to run he laughs already

les astres descendent familièrement sur la terre
C'est bien le moins qu'ils brûlent en se posant
la charogne noire des égoïstes

Les fleurs de ciment et de pierre
les longues lianes du fer les rubans bleus de l'acier
n'ont jamais rêvé d'un printemps pareil
Les collines se couvrent de primevères gigantesques
Ce sont des crèches des cuisines pour vingt mille dîneurs
des maisons des maisons des clubs
pareils à des tournesols à des trèfles à quatre feuilles
Les routes se nouent comme des cravates
Il se lève une aurore au-dessus des salles de bains
Le mai socialiste est annoncé par mille hirondelles
Dans les champs une grande lutte est ouverte
la lutte des fourmis et des loups
on ne peut pas se servir comme on voudrait des mitrailleuses
contre la routine et l'obstination
mais déjà 80% du pain cette année
provient des blés marxistes des Kolkhozes...
Les coquelicots sont devenus des drapeaux rouges
et des monstres nouveaux mâchonnent les épis

On ne sait plus ici ce que c'était que le chômage
Le bruit du marteau le bruit de la faucille
montent de la terre est-ce
bien la faucille est-ce est-ce
bien le marteau l'air est plein de criquets
Crécelles et caresses
URSS
Coups de feu Coups de couets Clameurs
C'est la jeunesse héroïque
Céréales aciéries SSSR SSSR
Les yeux bleus de la Révolution
brillent d'une cruauté nécessaire
SSSR SSSR SSSR
SSSR
Pour ceux qui prétendent que ce n'est pas un poème

the stars descend familiarly upon the earth
it's indeed the least which they burn in assuming
the black carrion of the egoists

The flowers of cement and of stone
the long creepers of iron the blue ribbons of steel
have never dreamed of such a spring
the hills are covered with gigantic primroses
they are homes for children kitchens for twenty thousand diners
houses houses clubs
like sunflowers like fourleafclovers
the roads are knotted like neckties
a dawn comes up over the bathhouses
The socialist May is announced by a thousand swallows
In the fields a great struggle opens
the struggle of ants and wolves
there aren't as many machineguns as we'd like
to use against routine and obstinacy
But already 80% of this year's bread
comes from the marxian wheat of the collective farms
the poppies have become redflags
the new monsters munch the ears of grain

Nobody knows here what unemployment was like
the noise of the hammer the noise of the sickle
mount from the earth is it
really the sickle is it is it
really the hammer the air is full of locusts
rattles and caresses
URSS
Gunshots cracking of whips clamours
It's the heroic youth
Steeled cereals SSSR SSSR
The blue eyes of the Revolution
shine with a necessary cruelty
SSSR SSSR SSSR
SSSR
For those who pretend that this is not a poem

pour ceux qui regrettant les lys ou le savon Palmolive
détourneront de moi leurs têtes de nuée
pour les Halte-là les Vous Voulez Rire
pour les dégoûtés les ricaneurs
pour ceux qui ne manqueront pas de percer à jour
les desseins sordides de l'auteur l'auteur
Ajoutera ces quelques mots bien simples

L'intervention devait débuter par l'entrée en scène de la Roumanie sous le prétexte, par exemple, d'un incident de frontière, entraînant la déclaration officielle de la guerre par la Pologne, et la solidarisation des Etats limitrophes. A cette intervention se seraient jointes les troupes de Wrangle qui auraient traversé la Roumanie...A leur retour de la conférence énergétique de Londres, se rendant en U. R. S. S. par Paris, Ramzine et Leritchev ont organisé la liaison avec le Torgprom par l'intermédiaire de Riabouchinski qui entretenait des rapports avec le Gouvernement français en la personne de Loucheur...Dans l'organisation de l'intervention le rôle directeur appartient à la France qui en a conduit la préparation avec l'aide active du Gouvernement anglais...

Les chiens les chiens les chiens conspirent
et comme le tréponème pâle échappe au microscope
Poincaré se flatte d'être un virus filtrant
La race des danseurs de poignards des maquereaux tzaristes
les grands ducs mannequins des casinos qu'on lance
Les délateurs à 25 francs la lettre
la grande pourriture de l'émigration
lentement dans le bidet français se cristallise
La morve polonaise et la bave roumaine
la vomissure du monde entier
s'amassent à tous les horizons du pays où se construit le socialisme
et les têtards se réjouissent
se voient déjà crapauds
décorés
députés qui sait ministres
Eaux sales suspendez votre écume
Eaux sales vous n'êtes pas le déluge
Eaux sales vous retomberez dans le bourbier occidental

for those who regret the lilies or the Palmolive soap
they will turn away from me their clouded heads
for the stop—there people the You're-joking people
for the disgusted people for the sneering people
for those who will not fail to put holes in
the sordid drawings of the author the author
Will add these few very simple words

Intervention should begin with the appearance of Rumania on
the scene, on the pretext, for instance, of some trouble on the fron-
tier involving an official declaration of war by Poland and the joining
together of the troops of Wrangel which would have traversed
Rumania...On their return from the energetic conference of
London, entering the URSS from Paris, Ramzine and Leritchev
have organized communication with the Torgprom through the in-
termediary of Riabouchinski, who was keeping up relations with the
French government personified by Loucheur...In the organization
of the intervention the chief role belongs to France which has pre-
pared it with the active aid of the English government...

The dogs the dogs the dogs are conspiring
and as the pale tréponème escapes the microscope
Poincaré flatters himself that he's a filtering poison
The race of the daggerdancers of the tzarist pimps
the dummy grand-dukes of the casinos which we lance
the informers who charge 25 francs a letter
the huge rottenness of emigration
slowly crystallizes in the French bidet
The Polish snot and the Rumanian drivel
the puke of the whole world
are massed on the horizons of the country where socialism builds itself
and the tadpoles rejoice
see themselves already as frogs
with decorations
deputies who knows ministers
Foul waters suspend your foam
Foul waters you are not the deluge
Foul waters you will fall again in the occidental slough

Eaux sales vous ne couvrirez pas les plaines où pousse le blé pur du devenir
Eaux sales Eaux sales vous ne dissoudrez pas l'oseille de l'avenir
Vous ne souillerez pas les marches de la collectivisation
Vous mourrez au seuil brûlant de la dialectique
de la dialectique aux cent tours porteuses de flammes écarlates
aux cent mille tours qui crachent le feu de mille et mille canons
Il faut que l'univers entende
une voix hurler la gloire de la dialectique matérialiste
qui marche sur ses pieds sur ses millions de pieds
chaussés de bottes militaires
sur ses pieds magnifiques comme la violence
tendant sa multitude de bras armés
vers l'image du Communisme vainqueur
Gloire à la dialectique matérialiste
et gloire à son incarnation
l'armée
Rouge
Gloire à
l'armée
Rouge
Une étoile est née de la terre
Une étoile aujourd'hui mène vers une bûche de feu
les soldats de Boudenny
En marche soldats de Boudenny
Vous êtes la conscience en armes du Prolétariat
Vous savez en portant la mort
à quelle vie admirable vous faites une route
Chacun de vos corps est un diamant qui tombe
Chacun de vos vers un feu qui purifie
L'éclair de vos fusils fait reculer l'ordure
France en tête
N'épargnez rien soldats de Boudenny
Chacun de vos cris porte au loin l'Haleine embrasée
de la Révolution Universelle
Chacune de nos respirations propage
Marx et Lénine dans le ciel
Vous êtes rouges comme l'aurore
rouges comme la colére
rouges comme le sang

Foul waters you will not cover the plains where sprouts the pure wheat of the
Foul waters Foul waters you will not dissolve the sorrel of the future   [future
You will not soil the steps of collectivization
You will die at the burning threshold of a dialectic
of a dialectic with a hundred turnings which carry scarlet flames
with a hundred thousand turnings which spit the fire of thousands and
The universe must hear   [thousands of canons
a voice yelling the glory of materialistic dialectic
marching on its feet on its millions of feet
booted with army boots
on feet magnificent like violence
outstretching its multitudinous warrior-arms
toward the image of triumphant Communism
Hail to materialistic dialectic
and hail to its incarnation
the Red
army
Hail to
the Red
army
A star is born on earth
A star today leads toward a fiery breach
the soldiers of Budenny
March on soldiers of Budenny
You are the armed conscience of the Proletariat
You know while you carry death
to what admirable life you are making a road
Each of your blows is a diamond which falls
Each of your steps a fire which purifies
The lightning of your guns makes ordure recoil
France at the head
Spare nothing soldiers of Budenny
Each of your cries carries afar the firefilled Breath
of Universal Revolution
Each of your breathings begets
Marx and Lenin in the sky
You are red like the dawn
red like anger
red like blood

Vous vengez Babeuf et Liebknecht
Prolétaires de tous les pays unissez-vous
Voix Appelez-les préparez leur la
voie à ces libérateurs qui joindront aux vôtres
leurs armes Prolétaires de tous les pays
Voici la catastrophe apprivoisée
Voici docile enfin la bondissante panthère
L'Histoire menée en laisse par la troisième Internationale
le train rouge s'ébranle et rien ne l'arrêtera
U R
S S
U R
S S
U R
S S
Il n'y a personne qui reste en arrière
agitant des mouchoirs Tout le monde est en marche
U R
S S
U R
S S
Inconscients oppositionnels
Il n'y a pas de frein sur la machine
Hurle écrasé mais le vent chante
U R
SS SS
SR UR
SS SSSR
Debout les damnés de la terre
S R
S S
S R
S S
Le passé meurt l'instant embraye
SSSR SSSR
les roues s'élancent le rail chauffe SSSR
Le train s'emballe vers demain
SSSR toujours plus vite SSSR

You avenge Babeuf and Liebknecht
Proletarians of all countries unite your
Voices Call them prepare for them the
way to those liberators who shall join with yours
their weapons Proletarians of all countries
Behold the tamed catastrophy
Behold docile at last the bounding panther
History led on leash by the third International
The red train starts and nothing shall stop it
UR
SS
UR
SS
UR
SS
No one remains behind
waving handkerchiefs Everyone is going
UR
SS
UR
SS
Unconscious opposers
There are no brakes on the engine
Howl crushed but the wind sings
UR
SS SS
SS UR
SS SSSR
Up you damned of earth
SS
SR
SS
SR
The past dies the moment is thrown into gear
SSSR SSSR
the roads spring the rail warms SSSR
the train plunges toward tomorrow
SSSR ever faster SSSR

En quatre ans le plan quinquennal
SSSR à bas l'exploitation de l'homme par l'homme
SSSR à bas l'ancien servage à bas le capital
à bas l'impérialisme à bas
SSSR SSSR SSSR

Ce qui grandit comme un cri dans les montagnes
Quand l'aigle frappé relâche soudainement ses serres
SSSR SSSR SSSR
C'est le chant de l'homme et son rire
C'est le train de l'étoile rouge
qui brûle les gares les signaux les airs
SSSR octobre octobre c'est l'express
octobre à travers l'univers SS
SR SSSR SSSR
SSSR SSSR

In four years the fiveyearplan
SSSR down with the exploiting of man by man
SSSR down with the old bondage down with capital
down with imperialism down with it!
SSSR SSSR SSSR

That which swells like a cry in the mountains
When the stricken eagle suddenly lets go with its talons
SSSR SSSR SSSR
It's the song of man and his laughter
It's the train of the red star
which burns the stations the signals the skies
SSSR October October it's the express
October across the universe SS
SR SSSR SSSR
SSSR SSSR

From *Literature of the World Revolution,* August 1931, and *Contempo,* III.5, February 1, 1933.

32

BALLAD OF AN INTELLECTUAL

Listen,you morons great and small
to the tale of an intellectuall
(and if you don't profit by his career
don't ever say Hoover gave nobody beer).

'Tis frequently stated out where he was born
that a rose is as weak as its shortest thorn:
they spit like quarters and sleep in their boots
and anyone dies when somebody shoots
and the sheriff arrives after everyone's went;
which isn't,perhaps,an environment
where you would(and I should)expect to find
overwhelming devotion to things of the mind.
But when it rains chickens we'll all catch larks
—to borrow a phrase from Karl the Marks.

As a child he was puny;shrank from noise
hated the girls and mistrusted the boise,
didn't like whisky,learned to spell
and generally seemed to be going to hell;
so his parents,encouraged by desperation,
gave him a classical education
(and went to sleep in their boots again
out in the land where women are main).

You know the rest:a critic of note,
a serious thinker,a lyrical pote,
lectured on Art from west to east
—did sass-seyeity fall for it? Cheast!
if a dowager balked at our hero's verse
he'd knock her cold with a page from Jerse;
why,he used to say to his friends,he used

"for getting a debutante give me Prused"
and many's the heiress who's up and swooned
after one canto by Ezra Pooned
(or—to borrow a cadence from Karl the Marx—
a biting chipmunk never barx).

But every bathtub will have its gin
and one man's sister's another man's sin
and a hand in the bush is a stitch in time
and Aint It All A Bloody Shime
and he suffered a fate which is worse than death
and I don't allude to unpleasant breath.

Our blooming hero awoke,one day,
to find he had nothing whatever to say:
which I might interpret(just for fun)
as meaning the es of a be was dun
and I mightn't think(and you mightn't,too)
that a Five Year Plan's worth a Gay Pay Oo
and both of us might irretrievably pause
ere believing that Stalin is Santa Clause:
which happily proves that neither of us
is really an intellectual cus.

For what did our intellectual do,
when he found himself so empty and blo?
he pondered a while and he said,said he
"It's the social system,it isn't me!
Not I am a fake,but America's phoney!
Not I am no artist,but Art's bologney!
Or—briefly to paraphrase Karl the Marx—
'The first law of nature is,trees will be parx.' "

Now all you morons of sundry classes
(who read the Times and who buy the Masses)
if you don't profit by his career
don't ever say Hoover gave nobody beer.

For whoso conniveth at Lenin his dream
shall dine upon bayonets,isn't and seam
and a miss is as good as a mile is best
for if you're not bourgeois you're Eddie Gest
and wastelands live and waistlines die,
which I very much hope it won't happen to eye;
or as comrade Shakespeare remarked of old
All that Glisters Is Mike Gold

(but a rolling snowball gathers no sparks
—and the same hold true of Karl the Marks).

From *Americana*, December 1932.

33

american critic ad 1935

alias faggoty slob with a sob in whose cot
tony onceaweek whisper winsomely pul

ling their wool over 120 mil
lion goats each and every one a spot
less lamb
            :nothing in any way sugge

stive
        ;nothing to which anyone might possibly obje

ct
    .& you know all he's got to do is just men
tion something & it sells ten 000 copies.won

derful.isn't it that poor man must read all the time.

read why i'd read in my sleep for half that mon
ey.you don't mean he.did i say anything again

st.wasn't that a.wasn't it.by what was the.such a funny name)

into which world is noone born alive

From *Townsman*, January 1938.

guilt is the cause of more disauders
than history's most obscene marorders

From *58 poèmes,* Paris 1958.

35

M   in a vicious world—to love virtue
A   in a craven world—to have courage
R   in a treacherous world—to prove loyal
I   in a wavering world—to stand firm

A   in a cruel world—to show mercy
N   in a biased world—to act justly
N   in a shameless world—to live nobly
E   in a hateful world—to forgive

M   in a venal world—to be honest
O   in a heartless world—to be human
O   in a killing world—to create
R   in a sick world—to be whole

E   in an epoch of UNself—to be ONEself

From *Adventures in Value*, New York 1962.

DOVEGLION

he isn't looking at anything
he isn't looking for something
he isn't looking
he is seeing

what

not something outside himself
not anything inside himself
but himself

himself how

not as some anyone
not as any someone

only as a noone(who is everyone)

From *Adventures in Value*, New York 1962.